Investigating STDs
(Sexually Transmitted Diseases):
Real Facts for Real Lives

Library of Congress Cataloging-in-Publication Data

Ambrose, Marylou.
    Investigating STDs (sexually transmitted diseases): real facts for real lives /
Marylou Ambrose and Veronica Deisler.
       p. cm.—(Investigating diseases)
    Includes bibliographical references and index.
    Summary: "Provides information about sexually transmitted diseases, including
    treatment, diagnosis, history, medical advances, and true stories about people
    with the diseases"—Provided by publisher.
    ISBN 978-0-7660-3342-9
    1. Sexually transmitted diseases—Juvenile literature. I. Deisler,
Veronica. II. Title.
    RC200.25.A43 2011
    616.95'1—dc22

                                                                            2008050061

Printed in the United States of America

052010 Lake Book Manufacturing, Inc., Melrose Park, IL

10 9 8 7 6 5 4 3 2 1

To Our Readers:
We have done our best to make sure all Internet Addresses in this book were active and appropriate when we went to press. However, the author and the publisher have no control over and assume no liability for the material available on those Internet sites or on other Web sites they may link to. Any comments or suggestions can be sent by e-mail to comments@enslow.com or to the address on the back cover.

Photo Credits: © Andrew Gray, p. 51; © Anka Grzywacz, p. 75; AP Photo/Seth Wenig, p. 25; CDC/C. Goldsmith, P. Feorino, E. L. Palmer, W. R. McManus, p. 91; CDC/Dr. Edwin P. Ewing, Jr., pp. 7, 53; CDC/ Hsi Liu, Ph.D., MBA, James Gathany, p. 92; CDC/James Gathany, pp. 10, 94, 100; Denver Public Health, Education Development Center, Inc., Mile End Films, San Francisco Department of Public Health, University of California San Francisco, p. 108; © iStock/Aldo Murillo, p. 136; © iStock/Ana Abejon, p. 43; © iStock/Chris Schmidt, p. 126; © iStock/Eileen Hart, p. 127; © iStock/Freddie Vargas, p. 135; © iStock/Jose Manuel Gelpi Diaz, p. 85; © iStock/Julie de Leseleuc; p. 12 (telephone); © iStock/Karen Town, p. 12 (girl); © iStock/kkgas, p. 83; © iStock/knape, p. 68; © iStock/Michael Krinke, p. 4; © iStock/Michel Rohner, p. 28; © iStock/Nancy Louie, p. 93; © iStock/Rhienna Cutler, p. 18; © iStock/Steve Cole, p. 21; Library of Congress, pp. 24 (Capone), 47, 57; Lupin Pharmaceuticals, Inc., p. 117; © Marcello Casal JR/Abr, p. 111; Merck, p. 39; Records of the Centers for Disease Control and Prevention/National Archives, p. 54; © Sanja Gjenero, p. 41; Shutterstock, pp. 3, 76; © SuperStock/George Goodwin, p. 37; The Stonesong Press, pp. 29, 30, 139; Trojan, p. 77; UNAIDS, pp. 124, 125; Veer, pp. 78, 95; WHO (World Health Organization), p. 101; WHO/WPRO/Image Bank, p. 122; Wikimedia Commons, pp. 24, 35, 48, 59, 130; © William Rafti, p. 34.

Cover Photo: Shutterstock

INVESTIGATING DISEASES

Investigating STDs (Sexually Transmitted Diseases):
Real Facts for Real Lives

Marylou Ambrose
and
Veronica Deisler

Enslow Publishers, Inc.
40 Industrial Road
Box 398
Berkeley Heights, NJ 07922
USA

Table of Contents

What Are STDs?

STD stands for sexually transmitted disease. It is a disease transmitted by sexual intercourse or any form of genital contact. STDs are a worldwide problem. The most common ones in the United States include chlamydia, gonorrhea, hepatitis B, herpes, HIV, HPV, pubic lice, scabies, syphilis, and trichomoniasis.

WHAT ARE THE SYMPTOMS?

Depending on the STD, some symptoms are fever, sore throat, fatigue, severe itching, rashes, sores and blisters, abdominal pain, burning with urination, discharge from the penis or vagina, or throat and eye infections. Sexually transmitted diseases are often without symptoms, too.

WHAT CAUSES STDs?

STDs are caused by having unsafe or unprotected sex with people who are infected with STDs.

HOW MANY PEOPLE HAVE STDs?

It is estimated that over 65 million people living in the United States are infected with a viral STD, and that 19 million new STD infections occur each year.

WHO GETS STDs?

Anyone who has sex can get an STD. They are most prevalent among young people (ages fifteen to twenty-four), women, racial and ethnic minorities, and gay men.

ARE THEY CURABLE?

Chlamydia, syphilis, gonorrhea, trichomoniasis, pubic lice, and scabies are curable, if treated. Genital herpes, chronic hepatitis B, HPV, and HIV are not.

ARE THEY PREVENTABLE?

All STDs can be prevented by avoiding unsafe sex. There are also pre-exposure vaccines available for HPV and hepatitis B.

Introduction

When people write about the problem of sexually transmitted diseases (STDs) today, they often refer to it as the "silent epidemic." That is because fear, embarrassment, shame, and social stigmas often lead people to take a vow of silence when it comes to talking about STDs.

It is time for a wake-up call. According to The Centers for Disease Control and Prevention—the federal government's top public health agency—about 19 million new STD infections occur in the United States every year and almost half of them are in the fifteen-to-twenty-four age group.[1] Worldwide statistics are harder to find because no single organization keeps track of them. But we know that the number of STD cases continues to grow, with hundreds of millions of new cases every year.

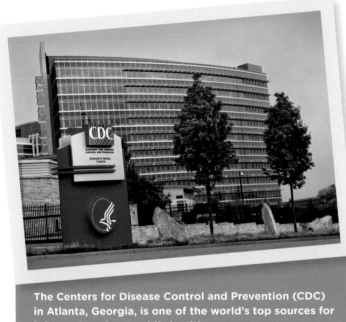

The Centers for Disease Control and Prevention (CDC) in Atlanta, Georgia, is one of the world's top sources for information about public health.

Sexually transmitted diseases have been around since history was first recorded, and they probably existed before that. But in spite of medical advances in diagnosis and treatment, the situation is getting worse, not better. Although STDs can be prevented, people still do not know enough about these diseases to avoid getting them.

Learning about STDs is challenging. Each disease has its own characteristics and complications. Even more difficult is the commitment each person has to make to either eliminate STDs or manage them in his or her life.

This book covers the most common STDs in the United States and world today, their symptoms, the tests used to diagnose them, and their treatments. You'll get answers to important questions about how to have safer sex and what to do if you or someone you know discovers they have an STD. This book will also show how real people deal with STDs. Knowledge is power. A world without STDs is possible if everyone does his or her part.

CHAPTER ONE

Straight Talk About STDs

H eather learned about STDs in high school but she never thought she could get one, let alone two. She thought only people who slept around got STDs.

Heather met Michael during her junior year of college, and they slept together a few times without protection. Then they lost touch. After Heather graduated, she decided to contact him again. They started talking on the phone and writing letters and became very close. A year later, she got a job in the city where Michael lived. "I had no intention of ever sleeping with him again," Heather says. "We'd become best friends and I didn't want to ruin our friendship."

One summer night, Michael visited Heather. They ended up having sex. A few weeks later Heather noticed a tingly feeling "down there." She told Michael about it and said she was worried because they hadn't used a condom. But he said, "I'm clean, I swear it, I'll take any test you want me to right now." He seemed so sincere, Heather told him never mind. After all, he was her best friend.

To Heather's relief, the tingly feeling went away. She and Michael had unprotected sex a few more times, and then she moved away at the end of the summer. But they kept in touch.

Unfortunately, the tingly feeling came back. In November, Heather

STDs can be hard to talk about, even with people you trust.

plucked up her courage and asked her doctor to test her for STDs. She breathed a huge sigh of relief when all the tests came back negative, meaning she was "clean."

Then a couple months later, Heather noticed some tiny white bumps on her vagina. She immediately went to the doctor. The diagnosis was HPV—genital warts! The doctor prescribed a cream to make the warts go away. The cream worked, but Heather was upset with the diagnosis.

"I cried myself to sleep every night for weeks," Heather remembers. "I went from a girl with very high self-esteem to a complete emotional wreck in a matter of hours. I felt worthless, disgusting, and unworthy of anyone's love."

Michael was no help. When Heather called him to report the HPV diagnosis, he just said, "Sorry, I didn't know I had anything." When Heather pulled herself together enough to do some research, she learned that the HPV virus may stay with you forever and can be passed on even after the warts go away. There is no test and warts are the only symptom. But not everyone who has the virus gets warts.

The more Heather read, the more she realized that her current symptoms didn't sound like HPV. The white bumps were gone, but she was still having the tingling sensation, and now she noticed a small sore on her vagina. So she looked at her test results from the year before and realized she had never been tested for herpes! She went to an STD clinic right away and got a herpes test. When the results came back positive for genital herpes, Heather was devastated for the second time.

During all this, Heather was dating a wonderful guy, Rob. She had already dropped the HPV bomb on him and he said it was not a problem. Now she had to drop the herpes bomb. All Rob said was, "Honey, it's okay. We always use protection, and I haven't caught anything. It's not a big deal." Heather could not believe he was so understanding.

Continued on next page

Continued from previous page

Even so, Heather's disease was emotionally upsetting to her. Her doctor prescribed an antiviral medication to treat the herpes. She takes it twice a day. She has not had another herpes outbreak, and that helps keep her from feeling depressed. Without the drug, she knows she probably would have had many more outbreaks.

About a year after her herpes diagnosis, Heather called Michael. He got tested, too, and he was positive. They still talk on the phone occasionally, but he will not discuss the infection. Heather says she wishes he would because sometimes she feels like he is her only resource. She did confide in two close girlfriends and it helped at the time, but they did not really understand because they had not been through what she had. Heather also joined an online support group, which she says helps a lot. She can talk on message boards with other people who have HPV and herpes and get up-to-date information on both infections.

"Knowledge is power," Heather says. But she wishes she had known three years ago what she knows now.[1]

UNDERSTANDING STDs

Sexually transmitted diseases date back to ancient times, and they remain a major health problem in the United States and worldwide. The Centers for Disease Control and Prevention (CDC) estimates that every year, 19 million new STD infections occur in the United States and nearly half of them are in the fifteen-to-twenty-four age group.[2]

Although STDs are widespread and affect people of all ages, races, and socioeconomic backgrounds, they are not well understood. Why? Because even though sex is a common theme in the media, many people cringe at discussing sexual topics in a serious way. They are afraid or embarrassed to ask their doctors, parents, teachers, or counselors for correct information on preventing STDs or do not know where to go for help if they think they have one. Consequently, many STDs are never diagnosed or diagnosed too late, after many more people have become infected.

Ignoring or not knowing the facts about STDs can have serious health consequences for sexually active people. Many STDs have no symptoms or only vague symptoms, so people may not realize they are infected. They can then unknowingly infect others. Some STDs are minor and curable, while others are extremely painful, chronic (long lasting), or even deadly. People need to learn how STDs are transmitted, how to protect themselves and their sex partners, how to recognize the signs and symptoms of STDs, and where to go for advice and treatment.

HOW ARE STDs TRANSMITTED?

Sexually transmitted diseases are infections passed from one person to another through sex acts: vaginal intercourse (inserting the penis into the vagina), oral sex (stimulation of the genitals with the mouth), anal sex (inserting the penis into the anus), or skin-to-skin contact with the infected area of a person who has sores or warts from an STD. The lubricated inner linings, or mucous membranes, of the genital area, rectum, or mouth must touch the vaginal secretions, semen, or blood of an infected person for an STD to be transmitted. Several of these infections can also be transmitted by nonsexual means, such as through a puncture or break in the skin (read more about this in Chapter 2).

TYPES OF STDs

How many STDs are there? Experts list up to twenty, although some of them are very rare in the United States. The most common STDs in the United States are chlamydia, human papillomavirus (HPV), and trichomoniasis. Other common STDs are gonorrhea, hepatitis B, herpes, human immunodeficiency virus (HIV), pubic lice, scabies, and syphilis.

Sexually transmitted diseases are caused by several different organisms, including bacteria, viruses, protozoa, and parasites.

What Are Bacteria?

Bacteria are one-celled organisms that resemble spirals, balls, or rods under a microscope. They are so tiny that thousands of them could fit on a pencil eraser! Ninety-nine percent of bacteria are harmless, and many are actually good for people, supplying vitamins, helping the body digest food, and destroying cells that cause disease.[3] One percent of all bacteria make people sick. Food poisoning and pneumonia are caused by bacteria; so are the STDs gonorrhea, syphilis, and chlamydia. These bacteria multiply rapidly in the body and can destroy tissue. They are also infectious, meaning they can be passed on to other people. Luckily, many types of antibiotics have been developed to kill bacteria or stop their growth.

Bacteria cause gonorrhea, syphilis, and chlamydia. Viruses cause herpes, hepatitis B, AIDS, and genital warts. Protozoa are microscopic organisms that cause trichomoniasis. Parasites are tiny animals that live off the infected person, called the host. The pubic louse and scabies mite are parasites responsible for pubic lice and scabies infections.

The most common STDs in the United States are chlamydia, human papillomavirus (HPV), and trichomoniasis. Other common STDs are gonorrhea, hepatitis B, herpes, human immunodeficiency virus (HIV), pubic lice, scabies, and syphilis.

What Are Viruses?

Viruses are tiny bits of protein that contain genetic material. They are even smaller than bacteria. They invade the body's cells, lodge there, and then reproduce wildly, eventually destroying the cells. Most viruses start reproducing as soon as they get into the cell, but a few lie dormant for weeks, months, or even years before they begin disrupting a cell's normal functions and causing illness.

Unlike bacteria, there are no "good" viruses, but some viruses are much more serious than others. The common cold is a virus that is not serious. The flu is a virus that can be serious in people who are very young, very old, or who have other diseases at the same time. Several STDs are also caused by viruses, for example, herpes and hepatitis B. All viruses can be passed on to other people.

Viruses are hard to treat. Some viruses mutate (change) when they are transmitted from one person to the next, so a drug that works for one person will not work for another. Antibiotics can kill bacteria, but have no effect on viruses. Medications have been developed to treat a few viral infections, such as the flu, herpes, and hepatitis B. But viral diseases continue to be some of the most serious infectious diseases known to man.

WHO GETS STDs?

Anyone who has had sex can get an STD—*anyone*. That includes teens, adults, gay and straight people, people with only one sex partner, people with many partners, and senior citizens. People who have sex at a young age have a greater chance of acquiring an STD. So do people who have a lot of sex partners and those who have unprotected sex—that is, sex without using a condom (rubber) or other type of barrier. More women get STDs than men because differences in anatomy cause infections to pass from men to women more easily. People who are poor and lack access to

STDs are not transmitted through everyday interactions such as hugging or shaking hands.

good health care also have a higher incidence of STDs.[4]

There are lots of misconceptions about STDs. Some people think you can get an STD from shaking hands with or hugging an infected person. That is a myth. Other people think only those with multiple sex partners can get STDs or that you can only get one STD at a time. Both are myths. And many teens think that having only oral sex protects them against STDs. This is untrue, and it's one of the most dangerous myths out there.

Some people think you can get an STD from shaking hands with or hugging an infected person. That is a myth.

WHY ARE STDs SO COMMON?

The common cold and STDs are alike in two important ways: People of all ages catch both of them every day, and both colds and some STDs are caused by viruses. But that is where the comparison ends. People catch colds by touching something that has cold germs on it and then touching their eyes or nose, or by inhaling droplets that contain cold germs when someone nearby coughs or sneezes. No wonder about 1 billion Americans have colds every year![5]

Sexually transmitted diseases are a lot harder to catch. People do not get them from just being in a room with an infected person. Compared to the common cold, STDs are not that contagious.

Why, then, are at least 65 million Americans living with viral STDs today? Why do more than half of all Americans get an STD sometime during their lives? Why do one in four teens in the United States have an STD? And why, by age twenty-five, have half of all sexually active people had an STD?[6] Here are some reasons:

Lack of knowledge: People are embarrassed to ask for advice on how to prevent STDs and ashamed or afraid to seek help if they think they have one. Some doctors may even be reluctant to offer advice. A study by the CDC found that during routine physical exams, most teens do not ask their doctors questions about preventing STDs. The researchers suggested that doctors be encouraged to bring up the subject.[7]

Underestimating or denying risk: When it comes to getting an STD, many people think, "It can't happen to me," a common saying that is a common misconception. Or they think their chances of contracting an STD are low because they only have one sex partner. True, having multiple partners increases a person's chance of becoming infected. But having only one partner, or one partner for several months at a time, does not make a person immune to STDs. If a partner had unprotected sex in the past with someone infected with an STD, he or she can pass the disease on to future sex partners. And partners believed to be faithful are not always so.

Not realizing they are infected: People unknowingly pass infections on to others because they do not recognize the symptoms of STDs, and because many STDs have only vague symptoms at first.

Lack of money: Many poor people cannot afford health insurance and do not know where to get proper, free, or inexpensive medical care.

More types of STDs: More infection-causing organisms are being discovered, so the number of STDs continues to grow. It often takes years to find effective treatments or cures for new STDs.

WORLDWIDE PROBLEM

No one knows how many people on earth have STDs because no single organization keeps track of worldwide statistics. We do know that the numbers continue to grow. The most current estimates were published by the World Health Organization in 2001 and were based on the extent of the STD epidemic in 1999. The organization reported that, in people between the ages of fifteen and forty-nine, there were about 340 million *new* cases in 1999 of four of the most common STDs: trichomoniasis, gonorrhea, syphilis, and chlamydia. Countries with the highest number of new cases were in South and Southeast Asia, sub-Saharan Africa, Latin America, and the Caribbean (in order of prevalence). The study also found

STD or STI?

Experts are debating whether sexually transmitted diseases should actually be called sexually transmitted *infections*. When a person is infected with a sexually transmitted bacteria, virus, protozoa, or parasite, he might not have symptoms or his symptoms might be so mild he misses them. A *disease*, on the other hand, implies that a person is sick and has apparent signs and symptoms. An STD is an STI that has advanced to the disease stage and caused damage to the body. All STDs are caused by STIs, but not all STIs progress to diseases. For example, some people with herpes or HPV never have symptoms but can still pass the infection on to others.

This book uses the more familiar term *sexually transmitted disease,* or STD, to describe both infections and full-blown diseases.

that STDs were more prevalent in urban areas, in young adults, and in unmarried people.[8]

Shockingly, of all the industrialized countries, the United States has one of highest rates of STDs in the world. To help put things into perspective, fifty to one hundred times as many people in the U.S. have gonorrhea than in Sweden.[9]

Shockingly, of all the industrialized countries, the United States has one of highest rates of STDs in the world.

TEENS AND STDs

People of all ages can get STDs, but teens are especially susceptible. Why? Because they have more sex partners and more unprotected sex than older people. This occurs in part because teens do not have enough information to make smart choices. The teenage years are a time for learning and experimenting, including experimenting with sexuality. The risks are multiplied if teens also experiment with drugs and alcohol, which lower inhibitions and make them more likely to engage in risky behavior, such as unprotected sex. Unless someone gives teens straightforward information on what causes STDs and how to prevent them, infection rates will continue to soar.

EFFECTS OF UNTREATED STDs

People who do not seek medical treatment for their STDs will surely pass the infections on to others, especially if the

Don't be afraid to talk to your doctor if you have questions about STDs.

What Are Chronic Diseases?

Chronic is an important medical term. A chronic condition usually develops slowly, lasts three months or longer, and may be incurable. Some chronic diseases are easy to live with, some cause only periodic symptoms that can be controlled with medicine, and others may put severe restrictions on a person's life. Herpes is an example of a chronic STD. The opposite of chronic is *acute*. An acute illness usually comes on suddenly, lasts for a short time, and is curable. Pubic lice is an example of an acute STD.

symptoms go unnoticed or are too mild to cause much concern. For example, fifty percent of men and seventy five percent of women with chlamydia have no apparent signs of infection.[10]

Bacterial infections, such as gonorrhea and chlamydia, are curable, but viral infections, such as herpes and HIV, are not. All STDs are treatable, and early treatment can reduce symptoms and help stop the spread of infection to others.

Even with treatment, the complications of some STDs can last a lifetime, and the damage is worse for women and their unborn babies. Untreated chlamydia and gonorrhea can lead to infertility in women and sterility in men. Mothers with syphilis can have babies who are born dead, die shortly after birth, or are born with brain damage and other deformities. Syphilis can also damage a person's heart, brain, and other organs and be deadly over the course of years. Human papillomavirus (HPV) may lead to cancer of the cervix (an internal structure at the top of the vaginal canal). Herpes can be passed from mother to baby during delivery. Some STDs can make a person more susceptible to getting other STDs, such as HIV.

LIVING WITH AN STD

Living with any disease is hard, but living with an STD can be even harder because of the social shame attached to these infections. A person who has an easily treatable STD, such as chlamydia, does not have to live with the disease long because taking an antibiotic will cure it quickly. People with viral infections such as herpes have a harder time. Treatment for herpes lasts a lifetime, and painful outbreaks of blisters may still occur despite taking antiviral medication. Even when herpes is latent, or inactive, a person can still pass it on to a sex partner. Viral STDs are not bad experiences people can put behind them. Sometimes, they are bad experiences that last forever.

For months, years, or the rest of their lives, people with chronic STDs must be vigilant about taking care of their health and preventing the spread of infection to sex partners. Women must take precautions to prevent infecting their unborn or newborn babies. In spite of these obstacles, millions of people with chronic STDs are living relatively normal, healthy, productive lives. Learning all they can about their disease helps people to accept its effect on their lives so they can stop dwelling on past mistakes and move ahead.

Once You've Been Cured of an STD You Can't Get It Again

Fiction! It is true that several STDs (chlamydia, syphilis, gonorrhea, trichomoniasis, pubic lice, and scabies) can be easily cured with medicine. But people can catch them over and over again if they have unprotected sex with an infected partner.

FAMOUS PEOPLE WITH STDs

The following historical figures are known or suspected to have had syphilis:

NAME	OCCUPATION
Vincent van Gogh (1853–1890)	Dutch painter
Napoleon Bonaparte (1769–1821)	French ruler
Al Capone (1899–1947)	Gangster
Howard Hughes (1905–1976)	Eccentric billionaire
King Henry VIII (1491–1547)	King of England

The following celebrities died of AIDS or are living with HIV:

NAME	OCCUPATION
Rock Hudson (1925–1985)	Film actor
Freddy Mercury (1946–1991)	Lead singer of British rock band Queen
Rudolph Nureyev (1938–1993)	Russian ballet dancer
Halston (1932–1990)	Fashion designer
Greg Louganis (1960–)	Olympic diver
Magic Johnson (1959–)	Professional basketball player

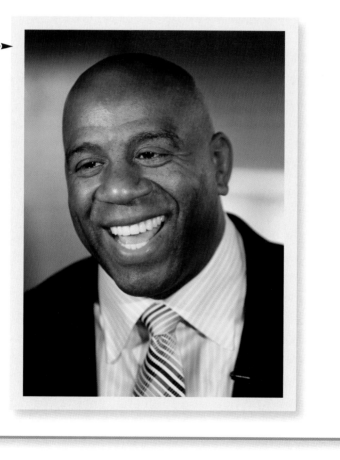

CHAPTER TWO

The Science of STDs

n 1945, when penicillin first came into widespread use to cure gonorrhea, people believed that all STDs would soon be wiped out. Sadly, that did not happen. Today, at least twenty different STDs exist, and new diseases and different strains of old diseases continue to be discovered. Some of these STDs cannot be cured, although their symptoms can be improved with treatment.

This chapter describes the ten most common STDs seen in the United States. It includes how people catch the diseases, what symptoms they have, what complications are possible, and more. Prevention, testing, and treatment are covered in Chapters 4 and 5.

CHLAMYDIA

Chlamydia (pronounced kluh-MIH-dee-uh) is caused by the bacterium *Chlamydia trachomatis*. It is the most common sexually transmitted bacterial infection in the United States, infecting an estimated 2.8 million Americans each year. People between the ages of fifteen and nineteen have the highest rates of infection.[1] The infection rate is three times higher in women than in men and seven times higher in African-American women than in white women.[2]

The good news is that chlamydia is easy to eliminate with antibiotics. The bad news is that three out of four infected women and half of all infected men never have symptoms so they do not get tested or treated.[3] This means they unknowingly infect others.

HOW REAL PEOPLE DEAL: A CASE OF CHLAMYDIA

Tori was fifteen when she started dating Jason, a smart, funny, affectionate guy who was two years older. He was only her second boyfriend, and she was still a virgin. She told him she was not ready to have sex, and for a while he was okay with that. But after a year, Jason started pressuring Tori. "I loved him, so I felt the time was right," she says.

At first, they used a condom, but then Tori went to a women's clinic and got birth control pills, so they quit using condoms to avoid pregnancy. "We trusted each other," she said.

Because she was on the Pill, Tori had to go for yearly gynecological check-ups at the clinic. "I hated them," she admits, "but I found out how necessary they are."

Shortly after one of Tori's check-ups, the doctor called and said one of her test results was abnormal. She had chlamydia. "I was totally freaked out—I didn't have any symptoms. I knew the only person I could have gotten it from was Jason," Tori says.

The doctor was understanding, offering Tori tissues while she cried her eyes out, then offering brochures and two week's worth of antibiotics. She explained that chlamydia was completely curable, but that if left untreated it could cause infertility. She said Jason also needed antibiotics and that they should not have sex until the infection cleared up.

"I felt so dirty," Tori says, "even though the doctor said chlamydia is pretty common." All she could think was that Jason had cheated on her. But when she confronted him, he insisted he had not. After talking on the phone for an hour, they decided he must have gotten the infection from his past girl-friend. He agreed to go to the doctor right away and get treated.

"He said he was really sorry for hurting me," Tori says. "I decided to believe that he had caught the disease before we met." She's unsure whether Jason contacted his old girlfriend or not.

Continued on next page

Continued from previous page

If she had it to do all over again, Tori says she would have insisted that Jason be tested for STDs before they had sex and then used a condom every time. The Pill only prevents pregnancy, not STDs. "Before deciding to have sex, girls should definitely think about the risks," Tori says. "I wish I had."[4]

People who *do* have symptoms usually get them five to ten days after contact with an infected person. Chlamydia can occur in the genital area from vaginal sex, in the anal area from anal sex, in the eyes from touching an infected area and then touching the eyes, and in the throat from oral sex.

Some common symptoms of genital area chlamydia in women are pain in the abdomen or pelvic area, milky or yellow mucouslike discharge from the vagina, burning with urination or more frequent urination, and bleeding between periods or after having intercourse. Common symptoms in men include burning with urination, discharge from the penis, an itchy feeling inside the penis, and redness at the tip of the penis.

Anal area chlamydia in both men and women can cause rectal bleeding, diarrhea, or pain during bowel movements. Chlamydia in the eyes can cause itching, redness, and pain. Chlamydial infection in the throat may cause a sore throat. Throat infections are more common in women who perform oral sex on infected men. Chlamydia does not cause sores and is not transmitted bykissing.

Pregnant women can transmit chlamydia to their babies during delivery, who then develop the infection in several areas. Chlamydia can also cause miscarriage (loss of the baby before the twentieth week of pregnancy), premature birth (before thirty-seven weeks), or babies with low birth weights.

STDs such as chlamydia can complicate pregnancy and infect newborns.

People who do not take antibiotics for chlamydia can end up with permanent health problems. Women can get pelvic inflammatory disease or have ectopic pregnancies, a life-threatening condition in which the fetus grows outside the uterus. Both of these conditions can cause infertility. Men do not usually have complications, but a few end up infertile from a condition called epididymitis or urethritis (infection in the urethra).

Male Genital Anatomy

The **penis** has two parts: the shaft (main part) and the glans, or head. The small slit at the tip of the glans is where both urine and semen come out through the **urethra** (yoo-REE-thruh). The urethra is a tube that connects to the **bladder**, which stores urine. The **seminal vesicles** (SEH-mih-nuhl VEH-sih-kuhlz) and **prostate gland** produce fluids that are ingredients in semen. The **vas deferens** (vas DEH fuh renz) are the tubes that transport sperm to the urethra from each **epididymis** (eh-pih-DIH-duh-mus), coiled tubes that store maturing sperm. These tubes are located behind the **testicles** (TES-tih-kulz), two oval-shaped structures that produce sperm and testosterone, the hormone that causes male physical characteristics to develop. The testicles are contained in a saclike structure called the **scrotum** (SCROH-tum), which keeps the testicles cooler than body temperature so they can produce sperm. The **rectum** is the end of the large intestine where solid waste is stored until it exits the body through the **anus**.

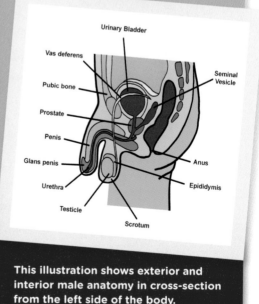

This illustration shows exterior and interior male anatomy in cross-section from the left side of the body.

Female Genital Anatomy

Internal anatomy:

The first structure in the internal genitals is the **vagina** (vuh-JY-nuh), a hollow tube that connects the outside of the body with the **uterus** (YOO-tuh-rus), or womb. The vagina is three to five inches long and has a mucous membrane lining that keeps it moist. It can temporarily expand to accommodate a baby during childbirth. Its other functions are for sexual intercourse and as the exit route for menstrual blood (the period). The **cervix** (SUR-vix) is located at the end of the vagina and is the opening to the uterus. The uterus is a pear-shaped organ about three inches long and two inches wide when a woman is not pregnant; it expands greatly during pregnancy to hold the growing baby. Its strong, muscular walls help push the baby out during labor. The two **fallopian** (fuh-LOH-pee-un) **tubes** connect the uterus to the two oval-shaped **ovaries** (OH-vuh-reez), located slightly above and to the left and right of the uterus. The ovaries' job is to make and store eggs and also to produce the hormones that cause female physical characteristics to develop. The other pelvic structures include the **bladder**, which stores urine, and the **rectum**, the end of the large intestine where solid waste is stored until it exits the body through the **anus**.

This illustration shows exterior and interior female anatomy in cross-section from the right side of the body.

External anatomy:
The **labia** (LAY-bee-uh) are the flaps of skin that surround the vagina. The labia minora (my-NOR-uh) are the inside folds of the labia majora (muh-JOR-uh). The **clitoris** (KLIH-tuh-rus), a tiny, very sensitive organ, is located above the vagina, where the two sides of the labia join. The opening of the **urethra** (yoo-REE-thruh) is located between the clitoris and vagina, inside the labia. It is the tube that transports urine from the bladder to the outside of the body.

GONORRHEA

Gonorrhea (gah-nuh-REE-uh), a bacterial STD, infects at least 700,000 people every year in the United States. Rates were declining until 1998, but they have been rising in recent years.[5] Gonorrhea is on the rise in young people, especially women between the ages of fifteen and nineteen.[6]

Gonorrhea is caused by the bacterium *Neisseria gonorrhoeae*. Because it is a bacterial infection, it is curable with antibiotics. Almost all men who get gonorrhea have symptoms one to fourteen days after exposure, but women may not. Gonorrhea occurs in the genital and anal areas from vaginal and anal intercourse and oral sex. It can also arise in the throat from oral sex and in the eyes from touching an infected area and then rubbing the eyes. Some typical symptoms of genital gonorrhea in a woman include abdominal pain, bleeding between periods, pain during urination or intercourse, and a yellowish vaginal discharge. Men often have a yellow discharge from the penis, burning during urination, and a feeling of irritation in the penis.

Anal infection can cause itching, pain with bowel movements, bleeding, and discharge. When the throat becomes infected, it may cause soreness or trouble swallowing. Gonorrhea in the eyes can cause redness, a thick yellow discharge, and vision problems. People cannot catch gonorrhea from a toilet seat or towel or through casual contact.

Untreated gonorrhea can lead to serious, permanent health problems. Men can end up with epididymitis, which can cause infertility. Women can get pelvic inflammatory disease (PID) or have ectopic pregnancies. Pregnant women can pass the infection to their babies during delivery, causing infants to become blind or have joint infections or life-threatening blood infections.

HEPATITIS B

Hepatitis (heh-puh-TY-tihs) is a whole spectrum of diseases (A, B, C, and more), but only one—hepatitis B—is commonly transmitted sexually. Hepatitis B is caused by a virus, so it is not treatable with antibiotics; however, a vaccination can prevent it or make it less serious.

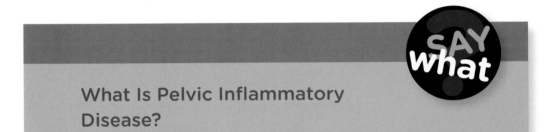

What Is Pelvic Inflammatory Disease?

Pelvic inflammatory disease (PID) is an infection of the female reproductive organs, including the uterus, fallopian tubes, and ovaries. It is caused when bacteria enter the vagina and travel into the reproductive organs. About eighty-five percent of all cases are caused by STD bacteria, especially gonorrhea and chlamydia. At least one million American women get PID each year.[7]

Symptoms include vaginal discharge that may have a foul odor, painful urination and intercourse, fever, and irregular menstrual bleeding; however, symptoms are often vague. Consequently, PID often goes untreated, causing 100,000 American women a year to become infertile.[8] The infection can also cause ectopic pregnancy and chronic (long-lasting) pelvic pain.

Pelvic inflammatory disease can be cured with antibiotics. Not having multiple sex partners and using condoms may help prevent PID.

What Is Epididymitis?

Epididymitis (eh-puh-dih-duh-MY-tus) causes swelling in the epididymis, a coiled tube inside a man's scrotum. This infection occurs when bacteria enter the urethra and then travel backward to the epididymis. Epididymitis is usually caused by chlamydia or gonorrhea, but it can also be caused by bacteria that are not transmitted sexually. More than 600,000 men visit a doctor each year to get treated for this infection.[9]

Symptoms include swelling, severe pain, and redness in the scrotum, almost always on only one side; burning during urination; and white, yellow, or clear discharge from the penis. Epididymitis it *not* caused by sperm or urine backing up when a man strains during urination. This is a myth.

Epididymitis can be cured with antibiotics. Waiting too long for treatment can result in infertility, because the function of the epididymis is to help sperm mature. Wearing a condom and not having multiple sexual partners can help prevent the infection.

According to the Centers for Disease Control and Prevention (CDC), about 60,000 new hepatitis B infections occur every year in the United States, and the number of people becoming infected is rising. Half of all people with hepatitis B get it from sexual intercourse,[10] and the more sex partners a person has, the more their risk increases. People who have or have had another STD are also at higher risk.

How do you spread hepatitis B? Sexually, by coming into contact with infected semen, vaginal fluids, blood, or urine through vaginal, anal, or oral sex. Even kissing is risky if the infected person's saliva contains blood. The infection can also be transmitted nonsexually, through sharing needles, using an infected person's toothbrush or razor, or by any other practice that puts someone in contact with blood.

Disease prevention mandates that needles be properly disposed of in an approved biohazard container, as shown in this photo.

Unfortunately, fewer than half of all infected people have symptoms. If they do, they get them six weeks to six months after infection. Early symptoms include profound fatigue, lack of appetite, pain and tenderness in the lower abdomen, nausea and vomiting, headache, joint pain, fever, and hives. Later symptoms include jaundice (yellow skin), worse abdominal pain, pale-colored bowel movements, and brown urine.

Out of twenty people with hepatitis B, one becomes a carrier and harbors the infection for the rest of his or her life, making the person more liable to transmit it to others.[11] These people are at a greater risk for liver disease. Liver failure and death occur in a very small number of people with hepatitis B. Most babies born to women with hepatitis B also carry the virus, but if they get vaccinated immediately, they almost always recover.

HERPES

A viral infection, herpes (HER-pees) is caused by herpes simplex virus type 1 (HSV-1) and type 2 (HSV-2). Both types can occur in the areas of the mouth, genitals, or anus. Infections around the mouth (also known as "cold sores" or "fever blisters") are called oral herpes and are most often caused by HSV-1. Infections around the genitals and anus are called genital herpes and are most often caused by HSV-2.

In the United States, at least 45 million adolescents and adults have genital herpes due to one of these two viruses. About one in four women and one in eight men have genital herpes caused by HSV-2.[12] Both types of herpes can cause blisters that break and leave painful sores.

People catch genital herpes by having vaginal, oral, or anal sex with someone who is infected. Most people do not realize that the virus that causes cold sores (HSV-1) can be transmitted to the genital area if a person with a cold sore performs oral sex on someone, and that the virus that usually causes genital herpes (HSV-2) can also be transmitted to the mouth during oral sex.

They also do not realize they can catch herpes from someone even if no sores are present. The virus lays dormant (quiet) in the spinal cord area for a long time and then becomes contagious when it travels along the nerves to the skin surface, where it can cause an outbreak of sores. But sometimes, the virus sheds without causing symptoms and no sores appear. So people may think they are not contagious when they actually are.

The herpes virus does not live long outside the body, so people cannot catch it from a toilet seat, towel, or drinking glass.

Many people do not even realize they have herpes because their symptoms are mild or they mistake them for something else. They may think they are having an allergic reaction to soap or that they have a bladder infection or yeast infection. Or they may have no symptoms whatsoever. When genital symptoms do occur, it is usually within two weeks after contact with an infected person. Besides the sores, people may have swollen glands, fever, and flulike symptoms. The first outbreak is often severe, with sores taking two to four weeks to heal. People may have several outbreaks during the first year, but they gradually get shorter and less severe. Before an outbreak, some people may notice tingling, burning, or itching in the area where they had sores before.

Cold sores are most often caused by HSV-1, one kind of the herpes simplex virus.

Genital herpes can cause serious complications, such as viral meningitis, an inflammation of the lining of the spinal cord, and encephalitis, an inflammation of the brain tissues. Luckily, both of these complications are rare. People with weakened immune systems, such as those with leukemia or HIV, have more severe herpes outbreaks. Herpes can also make people more likely to get HIV and make people with HIV more infectious.

Babies can get herpes from infected mothers, and these infections can be deadly. If a mother gets herpes while pregnant, this puts the baby at a greater risk than if the mother had herpes before pregnancy. If a mother has a herpes outbreak at the time of delivery, the doctor will usually perform a cesarean section—an operation that removes the baby through an incision in the abdomen.

Although there is no cure for herpes, antiviral drugs can prevent or shorten outbreaks. Not having sex during an outbreak and using a condom other times helps decrease the risk of contracting the infection.

HIV

Acquired immunodeficiency syndrome (AIDS) is caused by the human immunodeficiency virus (HIV), which attacks the body's immune system so it cannot fight off infections. The first cases of AIDS in the United States were reported in 1981, and today, the CDC estimates that 1,039,000 to 1,185,000 people in this country are living with HIV or full-blown AIDS. In 2006, about seventy-five percent of HIV and AIDS cases in adolescents and adults were in males.[13] Although both gay and straight people and people of all races get the infection, it occurs most often in men who have sex with men and in African Americans. However, heterosexuals and white men and women make up a large proportion of people infected with HIV, and these numbers are increasing.

Although there is no cure for herpes, antiviral drugs can prevent or shorten outbreaks.

The AIDS virus is present in blood, semen, vaginal fluids, and breast milk. It is most often spread through vaginal or anal intercourse or oral sex with an infected person or nonsexually by sharing needles or syringes during drug use. An infected woman can transmit HIV to her baby during pregnancy, birth, or breastfeeding. Urine, tears, and saliva contain a small amount of HIV, but unless they also contain blood, they do not transmit the virus. A person cannot become infected through hugging, kissing on the cheek, or other casual contact.

As this poster illustrates, HIV is *not* spread through casual contact.

You Can Get HIV from Kissing

Possibly. A peck on the cheek or a quick kiss with closed mouths is safe. But the AIDS virus is found in blood, so the CDC does not recommend open-mouth kissing with an infected person because contaminated blood could enter the other person's body through broken skin in the mouth.

Some people with HIV have no symptoms, but up to seventy percent have a sore throat, fever, or swollen glands shortly after they are first infected. These symptoms go away on their own in a few weeks, and then the virus can lie dormant for ten years or more.[14] People do not realize they are infected and may spread the virus.

The advanced stage of HIV disease is AIDS. Experts believe that everyone with HIV eventually develops AIDS, although some people stay well much longer than others. Eventually, HIV cripples the immune system so that people with the virus develop numerous health problems, including vaginal yeast infections, extreme fatigue, rapid weight loss, diarrhea, coughing, purple skin growths or other rashes, and confusion. Women with AIDS are also more likely to get cervical cancer than women without the disease.

Immune system breakdown leaves the body open to what are known as "opportunistic infections," which include certain types of pneumonia, tuberculosis, and severe and prolonged herpes outbreaks. Eventually, one of these infections kills the patient.

There is no cure for HIV or AIDS, but people who know they are infected can take a combination of drugs to boost the immune system and postpone the onset of AIDS.

HUMAN PAPILLOMAVIRUS

The human papillomavirus (HPV) is the most common STD in the United States. The CDC estimates that about 20 million Americans currently have the virus and 6.2 million more get infected every year. During their lives, at least half of all sexually active men and women become infected with HPV.[15]

The virus is transmitted through skin-to-skin contact, most often through vaginal or anal sex, but it can also be passed on by oral sex. The more sex partners a person has in his or her lifetime, the greater the risk of becoming infected. A pregnant woman can pass the infection to her baby during delivery, but this is very rare.

More than forty different types of HPV can infect the inner and outer genital areas of men and women. Most people have no visible signs or health problems, but some people develop one or more small, painless, flesh-colored bumps on the genital area, lower abdomen, or upper thighs. These are called genital warts and are usually caused by HPV types 6 and 11. Usually, warts appear one to three months after infection, but

Gardasil is a trailblazing vaccine to prevent HPV.

they may take years to occur. Sometimes, the warts go away on their own, without treatment, but people still have the virus. Or the warts might increase in size or number. Unless people have warts, they do not realize they have the virus and risk passing it on to sex partners.

In about ninety percent of all people, the body's immune system seems to fight off the virus within two years.[16] But experts are not sure whether the virus is actually gone or if the amount is just too small to be detected. In either case, people are not contagious. Unfortunately, the virus can reappear and be contagious years later if the person's immune system is weakened. Some things that can weaken your immune system are stress, other diseases, or poor health habits, such as smoking or poor nutrition.

Although most types of HPV cause little harm, two types (HPV 16 and 18) can cause cervical cancer in women. More than seventy percent of all cervical cancers are caused by HPV 16 and 18.[17] The vaccine Gardasil recently became available to help prevent these types of HPV as well as two other types that cause warts. Cervical cancer is curable if caught early. The HPV virus itself is not curable and stays in a person's body forever.

The risk of infecting others with HPV can be reduced by using condoms, although they are not as effective in preventing this infection as other STDs. That is because the HPV virus affects the whole genital area, and a condom only covers the penis. So having sex with a person who has HPV always has hazards.

PUBIC LICE

Pubic lice are miniscule insects that infest pubic hair, eyelashes, eyebrows, and underarm hair. They are also called "crabs" because they look like crabs under a magnifying glass. Every year, an estimated 3 million people become infected with pubic lice, most of them in their teens and early twenties.[18] Pubic lice are caused by the parasite *Phthirus pubic*. A parasite is an organism that lives off other organisms, and in this case, the lice live off the blood of the people they attach themselves to. They are extremely contagious and are transmitted by skin contact, usually sexual contact, although intercourse is not necessary. Pubic lice can also be spread through towels, clothes, or bedding. Catching lice from a toilet seat is possible, but unlikely, since the lice cannot hang on to smooth surfaces.

Not everyone with pubic lice notices symptoms. If they do, they may have severe itching, a low fever, tiredness, irritability, small spots of blood on their underwear, and tiny whitish or yellowish eggs (called "nits") attached to hair shafts. After they hatch, pubic lice are harder to see because they are tan or grey colored.

Getting rid of pubic lice on the body is easy and may be done with inexpensive, over-the-counter creams. All bedding, clothing, and towels used by the infected person should be washed in hot water and dried on the hot setting. Condoms do not protect against pubic lice. The best way to avoid getting pubic lice is to limit the number of sexual partners.

Towels and other shared linens must be laundered in hot water to rid them of pubic lice.

SCABIES

Scabies (SKAY-beez) is a highly contagious parasitic skin infection caused by the scabies mite, *Sarcopetes scabei*. This tiny insect tunnels under the skin and lays eggs, especially on the penis, buttocks, breasts, wrists, thighs, between the fingers, and around the belly button. No one knows how many people get scabies each year, but the infection is very common.

Scabies is spread by prolonged skin contact with an infected person. Adults usually get scabies through some type of sexual contact, although intercourse is not necessary. Scabies can also be spread throughout a household by sharing towels, clothing, and bedding. It is especially common in nursing homes, hospitals, day-care centers, or other places with crowded conditions.

Scabies causes small pimple-like bumps on the skin that appear in curling lines. Severe itching is common, especially at night. Symptoms usually develop two to four weeks after infection, although people who have had scabies before may start itching in just a few hours. There are generally only about ten scabies mites on the entire body, for reasons that aren't clear, so scabies can be hard to diagnose.

This infection is easy to treat with creams or lotions or with a pill. These medicines are not available without a prescription, so people need to see a doctor for diagnosis and treatment. All bedding, clothing, and towels used by the infected person should be washed in hot water and dried on the hot setting.

Condoms do not protect against scabies. The best way to avoid getting it is to limit sexual partners.

SYPHILIS

Syphilis (SIH-fuh-lis) is a common infection caused by the bacterium *Treponema pallidum*. It causes sores in the genital area and the mouth. In the United States, the number of people with syphilis peaked in the 1940s, but after penicillin was discovered, the numbers declined. In 2000, syphilis cases reached an all-time low, but since then, they have been steadily increasing every year. In 2006, U.S. health officials reported more than 36,000 cases of the disease, mostly in women aged twenty to twenty-four and men aged thirty-five to thirty-nine. That year, 64 percent of new cases of syphilis were among gay men.[19]

Syphilis is most prevalent in Africa and Southeast Asia. In the United States, more people have it in the South and in cities along the coasts. Poor people, people who use drugs, and people infected with HIV are especially susceptible to syphilis.

Doctors frequently counsel and seek to educate patients whom they have diagnosed with an STD.

This infection is spread through intercourse, oral sex, or touching an infected area, including kissing. It can also be spread from a mother to her unborn baby. You cannot catch syphilis from toilet seats, swimming pools or hot tubs, or eating utensils.

Syphilis occurs in several stages, and people are contagious during all of them. The primary stage occurs about twenty-one days after contact with an infected person and produces the classic syphilis symptom, the chancre (SHANG-kur). This small, round, painless sore appears at the location where syphilis entered the body. Usually, only one chancre appears, and many people do not even realize they have a sore if it is inside the vagina or the penis. Without treatment, the sore lasts for three to six weeks and goes away on its own. But then the disease progresses to the secondary stage.

Secondary stage syphilis occurs as the chancre is healing or several weeks later, when the infection enters the bloodstream. Symptoms include a red rash that covers the whole body, even the palms of the hands and soles of the feet, but does not itch; wartlike growths in the genital area; hair loss in patches; and fever, headache, tiredness, muscle aches, and swollen glands. However, some people have only a mild rash and may mistake their illness for the flu, especially when the symptoms disappear on their own. But this does not mean the infection has gone away. If people do not get treated, the disease will progress to the latent (hidden) and late phases. The latent stage of syphilis occurs when all the symptoms have disappeared. However, the bacteria are still in the body and the infected person is still contagious. The latent stage can last for years or for the rest of the person's life. About 15 percent of those with untreated syphilis progress to the late stage, which can occur ten to twenty years after exposure.[20]

In the late stage, the disease can damage the internal organs, including the brain, eyes, and heart. It can even be fatal. Luckily, late-stage syphilis is rare today because of antibiotics.

If syphilis is cured during the first two stages, the infected person has no lasting complications. However, mothers can pass syphilis to their unborn children during any stage of the disease. Infants may be born dead or die shortly after birth. If they are born without signs of the disease and do not receive treatment immediately, they can become blind, have seizures, or have other birth defects.

The latent stage of syphilis occurs when all the symptoms have disappeared.

Doctors in the United States and many other countries routinely test pregnant women for syphilis. However, many poor women or those without access to health care never see a doctor while they are pregnant, so some babies continue to be born with the disease.

Using condoms reduces the chance of getting syphilis, but chancres and other skin eruptions often occur in areas not protected by a condom, so there is still a chance of catching the disease from a chancre in another area.

TRICHOMONIASIS

Trichomoniasis (trik-uh-moh-NY-uh-sis) infects about 7.4 million men and women every year in the United States.[21] It is the most common curable STD in young women and probably the most common STD in the world.

The infection, often called "trich," is caused by *Trichomonas vaginalis*, a single-celled protozoan parasite. It occurs only in the genital area, not in the anal area or mouth, so it cannot be caught from oral or anal sex. It is easily transmitted through vaginal intercourse between opposite-sex partners or vulva-to-vulva contact between two women. Men and women can pass the infection on to other men and women, but men almost always catch it from a woman.

It is also conceivable that trichomoniasis could be transmitted in nonsexual ways, through genital contact with damp objects used by an infected person. For example, if a person shares a towel or bathing suit with someone who has trichomoniasis, they could catch the infection. But experts are still debating this theory.[22]

Trichomoniasis is the most common curable STD in young women and probably the most common STD in the world.

Most women who have trichomoniasis have symptoms, but most men do not. When men do have symptoms, they have a discharge from the penis, a need to urinate frequently, and pain and burning with urination. Women may have a yellow-green, fishy smelling vaginal discharge that contains spots of blood, itching inside and outside the vagina, and frequent urination with pain and burning. They usually get symptoms three to twenty-eight days after exposure.

The only complication of trichomoniasis occurs during pregnancy. Babies born to mothers with this infection may be premature or underweight. Babies may also become infected during delivery and catch genital or lung infections.

Trichomoniasis can be treated with prescription medicines. Using a condom decreases the chance of transmission.

The History of STDs

S exually transmitted diseases have been around for centuries, but what little is known about their history is mostly educated guesswork. Take herpes, for example. Lesions or sores resembling herpes were described on a clay tablet from 2200 B.C. The tablet belonged to the ancient Sumerian civilization which once inhabited southern Iraq. Similar lesions are mentioned in the Ebers Papyrus, an important Egyptian medical document from the 1500s B.C. Were these ancient lesions caused by herpes, or by some other skin disease that no longer exists? Medical historians can guess, but they cannot be sure.

The same is true for gonorrhea. A similar disease can be found in the Sumerian tablet and in early writings from China. The Ebers Papyrus suggests remedies for painful urination, which is a symptom of gonorrhea. Of course, it is also a symptom of a urinary tract infection (UTI) or a number of other medical problems.

Even the early Hebrews had their share of possible STDs. References to a man's "discharge" in the Old Testament may in some cases refer to gonorrhea rather than sperm. What about the plagues in Egypt and Moab? Could the scabs and itching described be the result of chancres and rashes? The Bible also mentions madness, blindness, and "astonishment" of the heart (heart failure), all symptoms of late-stage syphilis.

Hippocrates' work offers evidence that STDs existed in ancient times.

The ancient Greek physician Galen named the STD he observed "gonorrhea."

The Greeks and the Romans probably had STDs, too. The word "herpes" comes from the Greeks and means "creep" or "crawl." In the fourth century B.C., the Greek physician Hippocrates used the word to describe lesions that seemed to creep or crawl along a person's skin. The Roman emperor Tiberius must have guessed the disease was contagious. In the first century A.D., he banned kissing in public places to stop an epidemic of lip sores!

In the second century, a Greek physician called Galen gave gonorrhea its name. It means "flow of seed" because he mistakenly believed the discharge caused by the disease was an involuntary loss of semen. There are allusions to other STDs in ancient texts, including ones causing yellowish skin (a symptom of hepatitis) and itchiness (a symptom of scabies). Of course, many of these symptoms could be attributed to other diseases as well.

The most heated debate about the origins of an STD began during the Renaissance (A.D.1400 to 1600) in Europe.

The world "herpes" comes from the Greeks and means "creep" or "crawl."

THE ORIGINS OF SYPHILIS

Most people are convinced that gonorrhea has been around for a long time, but historians have been debating the origins of syphilis for 500 years. One theory holds that Columbus and his fellow explorers brought the disease back to Europe from the Americas (the New World) in the late 1400s. Shortly after their return, an epidemic of syphilis spread across Europe (the Old World), beginning in 1495. To add weight to the theory, modern archeologists have found evidence of syphilis in skeletons of Native Americans from 800 to 1600 years ago.[1]

A second theory argues that syphilis existed in the Old World from ancient times. The possible references to syphilis in the Bible (mentioned earlier) support this theory. So does evidence of bone lesions from the skeletons of English monks, dating back to the thirteenth and fourteenth centuries.[2]

The combination theory proposes that an earlier contagious species of the disease may have been carried across the Bering Strait when people migrated from Asia to the Americas thousands of years ago. When the New World disease collided with the Old World disease, it mutated into syphilis.[3]

Some people even believe that some historical accounts of leprosy (a disfiguring skin and nerve disease present since Biblical times) were actually describing syphilis and that the syphilis outbreak in the late 1400s merely coincided with Columbus's expedition.

AN EPIDEMIC RAGES THROUGH EUROPE

The origins of syphilis may be debatable, but it is fact that this virulent (deadly) disease spread like wildfire across Europe after 1495. It started after the siege of Naples. French soldiers had been fighting the Spanish there, but were forced to retreat when many of them became ill with a mysterious disease, probably caused by sex with prostitutes.

What Is an Epidemic? A Pandemic?

An epidemic occurs when a group or a region suddenly has more cases of a disease than usual during a given period of time. It is usually the result of a severe outbreak.

A pandemic is just like an epidemic, only on a larger scale. When an epidemic becomes widespread and affects a larger region, a continent, or the entire world, it is called a pandemic.

For example, HIV/AIDS first appeared in the United States in a small part of the population: gay men, drug users, and hemophiliacs (people who have a disorder that causes excessive bleeding). In a few short years, it spread quickly to others, creating an epidemic. Meanwhile, several other countries had their own epidemics of the disease. Now that HIV/AIDS has spread through the entire world, it is considered a pandemic.

As the soldiers returned home, they spread the infection throughout Europe. By 1502, syphilis was everywhere in Europe, and by the 1520s, it was recognized that the disease was sexually transmitted.

No country wanted to accept blame for the epidemic. People called it "the Italian disease," "the French sickness," "the Spanish disease," and the "great pox" (so no one would confuse it with smallpox). The name "syphilis" was eventually coined after a 1,300-verse poem written in Latin by Girolamo Fracastoro around 1530. The hero was a shepherd boy named Syphilis, who contracted the disease as a punishment for offending the gods. Looking at the disease as divine retribution was an indication of the poor view that people held of the disease and its sufferers, a view that still exists today.

OVER 300 YEARS OF CONFUSION

Scientists paid so much attention to syphilis in the 1500s that they neglected the other common STD—gonorrhea. Remedies to treat gonorrhea had been available for centuries, but most were useless. To make matters worse, the rise of syphilis in Europe caused confusion between the two diseases. Some scientists believed gonorrhea was the first stage of syphilis—probably because people often suffered from both at the same time. A British surgeon named John Hunter tried to prove they were the same in 1767. He supposedly inoculated himself with gonorrhea from a patient (who also had syphilis) and gave himself both diseases!

It was not until years later, in 1837, that French physician Philippe Ricord proved that syphilis and gonorrhea were two different diseases. He was also the first to describe the three different stages of syphilis. That led to the discovery that the third stage of syphilis could be latent and that it could also cause more serious diseases—of the heart, nerves, and brain—as much as twenty years later. It could even lead to dementia (insanity), paralysis, and death.

A statue of British surgeon John Hunter, who lived in the 1700s, stands at the Oxford Museum of Natural History in Great Britain.

A PERIOD OF GROWTH

The nineteenth century was a period of growth in understanding syphilis and gonorrhea, which were now called venereal diseases. The name "venereal" comes from the Latin expression, *morbus venereus,* which means "the sickness of Venus" (Venus was the Roman goddess of love).

For a long time, gonorrhea was considered a minor disorder compared to syphilis. That changed after 1879, when German dermatologist Albert Neisser discovered the bacterium responsible for gonorrhea and named it "gonococcus." Further studies showed that gonorrhea could cause arthritis, meningitis, and other serious diseases. Scientists began to take gonorrhea seriously.

The devastating impact that venereal disease could have on the family also became evident during this period. In 1872, American physician Emil Noeggerath discovered that gonorrhea could be latent in men but still communicable. That explained, Noeggerath said, "why so many healthy blooming young girls begin to suffer and fail as soon as they enter the bonds of marriage."[4] He also pointed out that women with gonorrhea infections frequently became sterile.

Earlier in the century, it was learned that the gonococcus bacterium could cause blindness in newborns. In 1881, a German obstetrician named Karl Credé discovered that infants were "infected only through direct transfer of the vaginal discharge into their eyes during the act of birth."[5] Credé knew that doctors had been using silver nitrate to treat ophthalmia (inflammation of the eye) since 1830. He found that instilling a two percent solution of silver nitrate drops into a newborn's eyes could prevent blindness.

Meanwhile, French dermatologist Alfred Fournier was studying the effects of syphilis on pregnancy and newborns. In 1883, he described a condition called "congenital syphilis," in which children are born healthy but suffer from the effects of the disease later in life. He demonstrated that children born with this disease were predisposed to meningitis, severe mental retardation, and other serious disorders. Progress had been made, but there were still no cures or treatments for the two diseases that were growing to epidemic proportions.

A MAGIC BULLET

Doctors had been treating venereal diseases for centuries. Everything from taking herbs to cauterizing sores with a hot iron had been tried with little success. Mercury ointments

Treponema pallidum spirochetes, the bacteria that cause syphilis, are visible through the microscope when dyed with a modified Steiner silver stain.

were a popular cure for syphilis. Since the chancre disappeared during the normal course of the disease, this cure was thought to be successful. But patients usually suffered less from the disease than from the "cure," because mercury is poisonous, and using it often led to serious complications, such as loss of teeth, cracks in the tongue, and bleeding of the bowel.

Thanks to advances in microscopic technology, a series of important breakthroughs occurred in the early twentieth century. In 1905, two German researchers named Fritz Schaudinn and Eric Hoffmann identified the bacterium that caused syphilis, a spiral-shaped microorganism they called *Treponema pallidum*. One year later, August von Wassermann developed a diagnostic test for syphilis. Finally, in 1909, Nobel Prize winner Paul Ehrlich discovered the first effective treatment for syphilis. He called it Salvarsan.

Salvarsan was an arsenic compound that he described as a "magic bullet" that could kill the bacteria, not the person.

HOW REAL PEOPLE DEAL: A SHAMEFUL EXPERIMENT

Charlie Pollard was only twenty-six years old when nurse Eunice Rivers came looking for recruits one Sunday afternoon in 1932. Poverty was a way of life back then in Macon County, Alabama. With an average income of two dollars a day, people could hardly afford to feed and clothe themselves, let alone pay for a doctor when they were sick. When Nurse Rivers offered the men free meals and free medical care, who could say no? What Charlie did not know was that he had signed himself up for one of the most shameful research projects in this country's history—the Tuskegee Syphilis Study.

For the next forty years, government doctors kept track of the 600 black men in the study, 399 of them infected with syphilis. Charlie was one of them. Every month the men were examined and every month they gave a sample of their blood. Most of them were semiliterate sharecroppers (tenants who work another person's land for a share of the crops), and none of them knew they had syphilis. Whenever someone was sick,

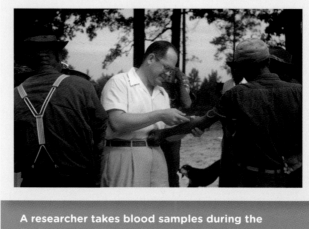

A researcher takes blood samples during the Tuskegee Syphilis Study in the 1960s.

he was told he had "bad blood," and that the doctors had come to treat it for free. Charlie was given little white pills, some salve to rub on his sides, and a "blood tonic." He thought he was getting treatment for his health.

The shameful part was that Charlie was getting no treatment for his syphilis. None of the men were. The purpose of the study was not to treat the "bad blood," but to see what would happen if the "bad blood" was *not* treated. Over the years, the doctors made certain that the men remained untreated. When penicillin became available after World War II, they were not given any. If any of the men attempted to go for treatment somewhere else, they were prevented from doing so.

Every four months, Nurse Rivers drove the men to the hospital in Tuskegee for more thorough exams, including an X-ray and, for a time, painful spinal taps. Charlie remembered the doctors holding him down. He had to stay in bed for a week afterward. His only reward was a free dinner before returning home.

Forty years later, the Associated Press wrote a story about Tuskegee, exposing it to the world. By that time, twenty-eight men had died from syphilis and another hundred from complications. Forty wives had been infected by their husbands and at least nineteen children had been born with it. Charlie was lucky. His symptoms were mild compared to those of men like his uncle Frank, who went blind.

After the study was exposed, the government paid $10 million to the men and their heirs and promised free medical care to those infected. Finally, in 1997, President Clinton apologized to the few surviving men on behalf of the United States government. Charlie Pollard was one of them. He was ninety-one. It was an apology sixty-five years in the making.[6]

Although Salversan was effective and safe for some people, it was also highly toxic to other patients who died as a result of the treatment. With his discovery, however, Erlich had ushered in the modern age of chemotherapy, the kind of treatment now used primarily to kill cancer cells.

WAR AND THE BATTLE WITH STDs

Since ancient times, sex hygiene and behavior have been a problem for the world's military armies. The First World War (1914–18) was no exception. A soldier away from home is often lonely, homesick, and looking for female companionship. The U.S. War Department created the Commission on Training Camp Activities (CTCA) in 1917 to develop recreation programs for the troops and instruct them about sex and venereal diseases.

The CTCA established a Social Hygiene Instruction Division to provide posters, pamphlets, and classroom lectures on venereal diseases. The primary message? Venereal disease could make an army less effective. A soldier who was sick could not fight. It was his patriotic duty to remain healthy. The division also stressed the dangers of soldiers infecting their wives and future brides with a venereal disease. (The army was male-only then.)

The CTCA did its best to remove temptation. It either closed down areas where prostitution flourished or prohibited soldiers from visiting them. Soldiers still had sex, however. Not always with prostitutes, but often with the many teenage "charity girls" who flocked to the camps in search of adventure and love.

Overseas in Europe, more practical means of prevention were put in place. Soldiers were ordered to sit through lectures on venereal disease, submit to medical examinations twice a month, and undergo treatments at prophylactic (preventive) stations within three hours of sexual contact.

The effort failed. Between April 1917 and December 1919, 383,705 soldiers were diagnosed with venereal diseases, costing the military 7 million days of active duty lost and 50 million dollars. Next to the influenza epidemic, venereal diseases were the most common illnesses among soldiers.[7]

During the Second World War (1939–45), medical officers realized that sex education could only accomplish so much. Posters with words like "Venereal Disease Helps the Enemy" were still displayed at army barracks and hospitals.[8] But the U.S. Army more openly promoted condom use and chemical treatments for those who were exposed to venereal disease, or VD as they now called it.

Pamphlets not only told soldiers how to avoid VD, but also told them what to do if infected. The Army even issued free condoms and individual prophylactic kits that allowed a soldier to treat himself if he thought he had a VD. In spite of these measures and improved medical treatments, venereal disease spread among the troops. The Army paid a huge cost in lost time and medical resources.

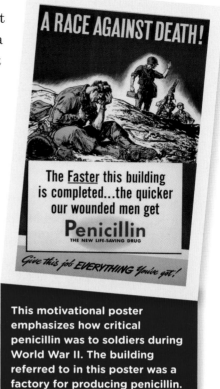

This motivational poster emphasizes how critical penicillin was to soldiers during World War II. The building referred to in this poster was a factory for producing penicillin.

Next to the influenza epidemic, venereal diseases were the most common illnesses among soldiers.

Syphilis and gonorrhea may have been the "dynamic duo" of venereal diseases until the 1940s, but other STDs have had a significant impact throughout history, too.

CHLAMYDIA

The dangers of STDs are not always apparent in the initial symptoms. Chlamydia is a perfect example. Both ancient Chinese and Egyptian manuscripts describe an eye infection that resembles trachoma, a contagious eye disease that can lead to blindness. In 1907, Drs. Ludwig Halberstaedter and Stanislaus von Prowazek infected orangutans with scrapings from the eyes of human adults with trachoma. What they discovered was the bacterium for chlamydia. They also learned it was contagious. The bacterium, which the men believed at the time was a protozoan, came to be known as *Chlamydia trachomatis*. Later, they observed it in newborns with ophthalmia (eye inflammation) that was not caused by gonorrhea.

In the 1940s, it was discovered that chlamydia also caused urethritis in men who, in turn, infected their wives. Pregnant women passed the infection on to the eyes of their babies during delivery—the source of the non-gonorrheal ophthalmia that Drs. Halberstaedter and Prowazek had observed. By 1990, a wide number of problems, such as PID and infertility, were found to be associated with chlamydia infection.

HEPATITIS

Hippocrates was the first to describe hepatitis around 400 B.C. Its infectious nature was documented during the eighth century A.D. During the 1600s and 1700s, outbreaks of hepatitis during wartime suggested that it could be transmitted through blood transfusions and syringes. Similar outbreaks during World War II confirmed the theory.

In 1908, researcher S. McDonald theorized that the jaundice seen in hepatitis was caused by a virus. He was right. In 1947, British physician F.O. MacCallum discovered two forms of the virus. Viral hepatitis A was carried by food and water infected with fecal matter. Viral hepatitis B was transferred by exposure to blood. Only hepatitis B could be spread through sexual contact, although some findings indicate that the sexual transmission of viral hepatitis C—identified in 1989—may be possible. Hepatitis C is also spread by exposure to blood and is the most common cause of chronic hepatitis.

HERPES

The Greeks and Romans were not the only ones worried about herpes. Shakespeare also probably had experience with the disease. In his play about two teenagers in love, *Romeo and Juliet*, first printed in 1597, he wrote about "ladies lips" that were plagued with "blisters" when they dreamed about kissing.

In 1736, John Astruc, a physician for King Louis XIV of France, found a connection between herpes and the genital organs while studying French prostitutes and their diseases. Emile Vidal took it one step further in the late 1800s. He proved herpes could be passed from person to person. Unfortunately, he did it by transferring the infection from one human to another—not an uncommon practice in the scientific experiments of the late nineteenth century.

The herpes simplex virus (HSV) was identified in 1919 by a researcher named Lowenstein (his first name is not available) who confirmed it was infectious by passing it on to rabbits. In the 1920s and 1930s, it was discovered that HSV also in-fected the central nervous sys-tem and could be latent. Finally, in 1962, it was classified into two types of virus, HSV-1 and HSV-2.

Louis XIV, shown above, had the best of everything, including a doctor who was at the forefront of the studies of STDs in eighteenth-century France.

HIV AND AIDS

The history of AIDS in the United States is brief but alarming. The disease was first recognized in this country in 1981. Gay men in New York and California were developing infections and cancers that seemed resistant to any treatment. Similar cases were reported later among drug users, Haitians, and hemophiliacs (people with a disorder that causes excessive bleeding and requires blood transfusions). In 1982, the mysterious disease was given a name: Acquired Immune Deficiency Syndrome, or AIDS.

No one really knows the exact origins of AIDS, but there are numerous theories.

Advances in understanding AIDS moved as swiftly as the disease spread. In 1983, doctors at the Pasteur Institute in France identified the retrovirus (a virus composed of RNA instead of DNA) that caused AIDS. In 1985, a blood test was developed to diagnose the virus, and in 1986, it was named human immunodeficiency virus, or HIV. In that same year, nearly 3,000 people died in the United States from the disease. By 1995, the number of deaths had risen to over 48,000.[9] The country had an epidemic on its hands.

No one really knows the exact origins of AIDS, but there are numerous theories. Researchers discovered in 1999 that HIV-1 (the most common cause of AIDS in the United States) was similar to a virus called SIV found in chimpanzees in Africa. How was the disease transferred to humans? The most common theory is that humans killed and ate the diseased chimps, or the blood of the chimps got into the hunter's wounds.

The virus later mutated into HIV-1, then may have transferred from person to person by means of contaminated syringes. It is believed that African healthcare professionals might have reused syringes during inoculation programs in order to keep down costs.

Another theory argues that African laborers who were ruled by colonial forces during the late nineteenth and early twentieth century may have spread the infection, especially in French Equatorial Africa and the Belgian Congo where conditions were particularly harsh. Laborers in the camps ate poorly, and a chimp would have been welcome food. The physical demands on the laborers and poor sanitation would have already weakened their immune systems. Many of the laborers also could have been inoculated with unsterile needles, and the camps were known to employ prostitutes for the workers. Fifty percent of the labor camp populations were eventually wiped out by HIV. HIV is believed to have passed to humans during the time these labor camps were set up, so it could explain how the original infection became an epidemic.

Author and AIDS scholar Edward Hooper has another theory. He suggests that HIV can be traced to an oral polio vaccine called Chat that was cultivated in the living tissue of chimps infected with SIV. The vaccine was given to about a million people in the Belgian Congo and Ruanda-Urundi (later Rwanda and Burundi) in the late 1950s.[10]

However the HIV virus developed, it seems likely that Africa was where it originated and first spread. In 2007, scientists presented data showing that HIV-1 was brought to Haiti from the Congo by a single person around 1966. Probably another single individual brought the virus to United States between 1969 and 1972. Eventually, the virus took hold in the human population.

HUMAN PAPILLOMAVIRUS

Genital warts have been recognized as an STD since the early Greek and Roman eras. For centuries, people believed the warts were caused by syphilis or gonorrhea. Finally, in 1907, the Italian scientist Ciuffo was the first to identify genital warts as caused by a separate virus. As molecular biology advanced, it enabled researchers to identify human papillomavirus (HPV), just as it was taking hold in the human population.

Genital warts may be a relatively benign symptom of HPV, but the disease has more serious consequences. In the 1970s, German virologist Harald zur Hausen discovered that HPV was not one virus, but a family of viruses, and that two of them caused cervical cancer in women. Zur Hausen's discovery led to a search for an HPV vaccine.

PUBIC LICE

Recent DNA research has concluded that humans got pubic lice from apes over 3 million years ago.[11] How that happened is anyone's guess! The oldest fossil remains of pubic lice are from first- or second-century Britain. Remains of the crab-shaped lice have also been found in archeological deposits from seventeenth-century Iceland and eighteenth-century London.

Pubic lice may be more of a nuisance than a danger. Since they are spread through sexual contact, they serve as a warning that other STDs may be present. Studying these ancient insects can teach scientists how diseases develop and how parasites spread from one species to another.

SCABIES

Also known as the "itch mite," scabies dates back more than 2,500 years to the Greeks and Romans. St. Hildegard (1099–1179) was the first to officially discover the mite during

"CURES" AND FOLK REMEDIES FOR STDs

Attitudes toward sexual activity can be complicated. In the past, society did not make it easy for people with STDs, often treating them as if they had done something wrong. Going back to ancient times, physicians frequently invented cures that would teach the patient a painful lesson.

For example, the ancient Greek physician Celsus suggested treating herpes by burning the sores with a hot iron. During the 1500s, patients drank a solution made from guaiacum wood to induce sweating. They also had to stay in a hot room and fast for forty days. Some of the more absurd folk cures have involved smothering with pillows, transferring the disease to a virgin or a donkey, and praying to patron saints.

But nothing compares to the 1900s for making a patient pay for his or her "sin." One physician suggested injecting quarts of hot water (180° F) into the infected area—until *after* the patient could no longer tolerate the pain.

Mercury, an early remedy for syphilis, caused patients to salivate, which supposedly removed the syphilitic poison from the body. It also made their teeth loose, bones soft, hair fall out, and caused sores to develop on their mouth, tongue, and throat. That is, if they were lucky enough not to die from mercury poisoning.

One doctor's solution for curvature of the penis (caused by gonorrhea) was to flatten the organ by placing it on a table and striking it violently with a book! Convinced that gonorrhea was the result of excessive sexual intercourse, many nineteenth-century doctors recommended (without much logic) marriage as a cure.

By the end of the nineteenth century, physicians were better informed and abandoned these punishing efforts to "cure" their patients. The emphasis switched to the treatment of STDs, but the moral stigma still lingers today.

the Middle Ages. She left writings about the different skin diseases she observed, including scabies. Her recommended treatment was sulfur ointment for five days. Hildegard also gave the disease a name: snebelza.

In 1687, Giovan Bonomo drew a picture of the mite that caused scabies and described it as "a minute living creature . . . with six feet, a sharp head, with two little horns at the end of the snout."[12] Not a pleasant sight!

In 1805, Joseph Adams wanted to prove that the mite truly caused scabies. So he did what any good scientist would do. He infected himself with it! It was no surprise when, two weeks later, his skin erupted in lesions and he started to itch.

Today, the term *scabies* refers to the skin lesions caused by the mite. Scabies is still difficult to diagnose and often goes untreated because of it. In fact, the expression "7-year itch" was first used to describe this persistent and irritating disease. Later, it came to mean something entirely different, but originally it referred to scabies.

TRICHOMONIASIS

In 1836, the French physician Alfred Donné discovered the cause of trichomoniasis. It was a single-celled protozoan parasite he found in the genital secretions of infected men and women. He named it *Trichomonas vaginalis*. The disease was proved infectious in women in 1942 and in men in 1953.

PENICILLIN AND OTHER ANTIBIOTICS

Penicillin was touted as a miracle drug in the late 1920s, but since then, many other drugs have been developed to work miracles in curing and treating STDs. Penicillin was discovered by accident in 1928. A Scottish scientist named Alexander Fleming left a culture plate with bacteria in his lab while he was away on a vacation. He returned to discover that a mold had contaminated the plate. When Fleming saw that the bacteria filled the plate, except for the area around the mold, he had an "aha!" moment. Something in the mold had prevented the bacteria from growing. He called the active ingredient penicillin. It became the first antibiotic.

In 1940, British scientists Howard Florey and Ernst Chain purified Fleming's mold, developing its antibiotic nature, and successfully treated mice that were infected with deadly bacteria. The drug was extremely effective, but the problem then became making the new drug in large enough quantities. Pressed by the overwhelming casualties of World War II, they convinced the U.S. pharmaceutical companies to pitch in. By the end of the war, enough penicillin was made to save millions of lives and become a cure for syphilis, gonorrhea, and other deadly diseases. A "wonder drug" had been born.

Other antibiotics followed. Chlamydia, for example, is treated by azithromycin and doxycycline. Metronidazole is the treatment of choice for trichomoniasis. Several antibiotics are used to cure gonorrhea also. Unfortunately, antibiotic-resistant strains of gonorrhea are on the rise, making it more of a challenge to treat the disease. Antibiotic resistance arises when bacteria mutate (change) so that drugs developed to kill the old bacteria no longer work.

AIDS DRUGS

HIV's targets are the cells of the immune system that are supposed to protect the body against disease. After the virus enters a cell, it reproduces over and over again. Then it spreads to new cells until the immune system is destroyed. Most HIV drugs try to stop the virus from reproducing.

In 1987, six years after the first cases of AIDS were found in the United States, the FDA approved a drug named azidothymidine (AZT) to fight the new disease. During the next few years, similar drugs were added to the arsenal. They were somewhat effective, but results varied and many patients became resistant to them.

As new classes of drugs were developed over time, another therapy emerged—using two or more types of drugs at the same time. This combination therapy showed dramatic results. It helped to delay progression of the disease and prolong life. By 1997, it was the standard of care for many patients.

There are now six classes of drugs approved by the FDA and taken in combination to treat AIDS patients. In 2006, the first one-a-day pill, combining three drugs in a "cocktail," was approved for sale in the United States.

HERPES DRUGS

Genital herpes has been on the rise since the 1970s. In the past, it was diagnosed by visually inspecting sores or by taking a lab culture of an active sore. Today it is possible to diagnose herpes with a blood test, although these are often unreliable.

A new concern is growing evidence that people with herpes may be at greater risk for getting HIV. There is no cure for herpes. There are, however, antiviral medications, such as acyclovir, that can prevent or shorten herpes outbreaks.

HPV VACCINE

Although there is no treatment for the virus, a vaccine to prevent HPV—and most cervical cancers—has been discovered. Back in 1842, an Italian named Rigoni-Stern theorized that cervical cancer was sexually transmitted. He based his theory on the observation that nuns had virtually no cases of cervical cancer, while prostitutes had unusually high rates.

During the 1970s, Harald zur Hausen tested that theory with HPV. He proved that HPV 16 was present in about half of cervical cancer biopsies and that HPV 18 was present in another 17 to 20 percent. Zur Hausen shared his work with pharmaceutical companies to help them develop a vaccine against HPV. After more than two decades of research and several studies, a vaccine was finally approved by the FDA in 2006.

Today, more is known about STDs than the Greeks, Romans, or Shakespeare could have dreamed. There is still, however, much more to discover. Studying the histories of STDs and learning from them is a good place to start.

CHAPTER FOUR

Preventing STDs

Preventing an STD was once a matter of trial and error, because not much was known about transmission. But with all the useful information people have today about STDs, prevention should be a piece of cake. In fact, the number of cases should be going down every year, right? The sad reality is the opposite is true.

According to the CDC, an estimated 2,800,000 people become infected with chlamydia each year in the United States.[1] Between 2005 and 2006, the number of gonorrhea cases rose 5.5 percent. Syphilis infections increased 13.8 percent in the same time period. That accounts for the cases reported to the CDC. Estimates of unreported cases more than double those numbers.[2]

There are no statistics about increases per year in herpes, hepatitis B, HPV, and trichomoniasis yet. Annual estimates, however, are overwhelming: 1 million for herpes, 60,000 for hepatitis B, over 6 million for HPV, and 7.4 million for trichomoniasis. Although STDs affect everyone, the incidence is much higher among certain groups: women, infants of infected mothers, teens, young adults, and African Americans.[3] In 2005, African Americans made up about sixty-eight percent of the gonorrhea cases reported to

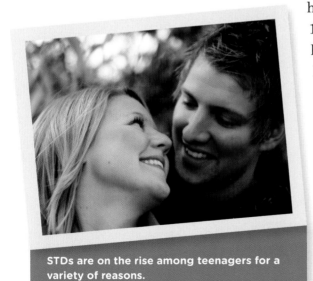

STDs are on the rise among teenagers for a variety of reasons.

the CDC. The same year, blacks had a chlamydia rate over eight times higher than whites.[4] It does not take much to see that STDs are still a serious problem.

WHY ARE STDs ON THE RISE?

Why? For starters, people do *not* want to talk about their STDs. The reasons are explained in Chapter 1: embarrassment, fear of criticism, denying risk, not realizing they are infected, lack of money, and worst of all, lack of knowledge. When people avoid treatment, unfortunately, they add to the probability of spreading STDs.

There are plenty of reasons for the increase in STDs among teenagers. Today's teens are more likely to have sex at an earlier age than in the past. They are also likely to have unprotected sex. In 2005, the CDC found that forty-seven percent of high school students admitted to having had sexual intercourse, fourteen percent of them had four or more sex partners, and thirty four percent had failed to use a condom during their most recent sexual intercourse.[5]

Social issues also contribute to the rise of STDs. Lack of self-esteem, emotional problems, and depression—especially among girls and women—are all linked to risky sexual behavior. People often try to fill the void with sex, mistaking it for love. What they may get instead is an STD.

People "in love" often add to the problem. They may start the relationship protected, but love blinds them after a while. How could someone they trust have an STD? As one researcher put it, "once you get past the first couple of weeks, the condoms usually go out the window."[6]

WHAT BEHAVIORS PUT PEOPLE AT RISK?

People take risks every day and for lots of good reasons. But there is no good reason to take a sexual risk, especially one that is dangerous to your health. No matter how intense the pressure from society, peers, and partners can get, there are certain risky behaviors everyone should avoid.

The number one risky behavior? Having unprotected sex. Unprotected sex includes vaginal, oral, *and* anal sex. In other words, a person can get an STD without having intercourse. The only safe way to avoid STDs is *not* to have sex, or to be in a long-term mutually monogamous (agreeing to have sex only with each other) relationship with a partner who has been tested and is free of STDs.

The number one risky behavior? Having unprotected sex. Unprotected sex includes vaginal, oral, *and* anal sex. In other words, a person can get an STD without having intercourse.

Starting young is another risk factor. A 2008 study estimated that twenty-six percent of girls in the United States between the ages of fourteen and nineteen were infected with at least one of the following: HPV, chlamydia, herpes, or trichomoniasis. Young women especially are more vulnerable to STDs. Their bodies are smaller, making them more likely to experience tearing during intercourse. Since their cervixes are not fully developed, they are also more vulnerable to chlamydia, gonorrhea, or other STDs. That is because the type of cells that are susceptible to STD infection can be found on the outer surface of a younger woman's cervix (ectocervix) instead of only on the inside of the cervix (endocervix). The condition is called "cervical ectopy." Some amount of ectopy is normal during puberty and usually decreases with aging.

Having multiple partners is also risky. It makes sense that the more partners a person has, the greater his or her chance of being exposed to an STD. The same 2008 study found that girls with three or more partners had an STD rate of over fifty percent.[7]

Taking drugs or alcohol before sex can lower inhibitions and lead to risky behavior. In one survey, twenty-three percent of students who had engaged in sexual intercourse over the past three months admitted to using drugs or drinking alcohol first.[8] Drugs and alcohol can also make it trickier to put on that condom!

Living in an area that has a high incidence of STDs leaves someone more exposed to the possibility of infection. So does sharing needles and exchanging sex for money. People who engage in risky behavior—multiple partners, injected drug use, or sex for money—are probably a risk themselves.

The final and most obvious risk is having sex with someone you know has an STD. Many people are not aware that if both partners have an STD, the risk factor is even greater. People who already have STDs can be more easily infected by other STDs. That is why getting tested before having sex is so important.

HOW TO PREVENT STDs

Just about everyone knows that having unprotected sex with an infected partner can give you an STD. Then why do so many people get STDs every year? The answer is simple. They are lacking the necessary information about how STDs spread and how they can be prevented. Knowing the kinds of behaviors that will make sex safer can make all the difference.

ABSTINENCE

The only effective way to avoid STDs hundred percent of the time is to say "no" to sex—all sex. Some people abstain forever. Other people say no until they feel they are ready to have sex. Still other people abstain from sex for different reasons and at different times in their lives. Many teens today take "virginity pledges"—pledges to abstain from sex until they are married.

What does it mean to abstain from sex? To abstain means to "avoid something by your own choice." So what does "sex" mean? Is it vaginal intercourse? Does it include oral sex? What about mutual masturbation? The last two acts are not sex to some people, but all three of them can transmit STDs.

One five-year study showed that 4.6 percent of teens who were consistent virginity pledgers had chlamydia, trichomoniasis, or gonorrhea at the end of the study. The non-pledgers had a

What Is Case Reporting?

How does the CDC know how many people have different STDs? By a process called case reporting. In every state, doctors' offices and laboratories are legally required to report definite or suspected cases of syphilis, gonorrhea, chlamydia, HIV, and AIDS either to local or state health departments, which, in turn, report the cases to the CDC. All reports are kept strictly confidential. Unfortunately, many doctors do not understand reporting rules or do not take the time to report STDs. Consequently, the actual number of cases is much higher than what is reported, which explains why the words "estimated" and "underreported" appear so often when STD statistics are discussed.

6.9 percent rate. Also, sixty-one percent of pledgers said they had intercourse by the end of the study or before they married.[9] Abstinence has to be perfect to work. Young people who choose that route need to be informed about other options, too, for their own safety.

CONDOMS

If saying no to sex is not an option, sex with condoms is the only way to go. Condoms cannot give you 100 percent protection from STDs, but they can reduce your risk. It is important to realize that risk reduction is not risk elimination. Condoms must be used the right way, every time you have sex. Studies show that people using latex condoms *correctly and consistently* during vaginal sex can reduce their risk of HIV by 85 percent. The risk for genital herpes and syphilis is reduced only when the infected areas are also covered or protected by a condom.[10] Whether or not condoms can prevent HPV is unknown, but using them has been associated with a lower incidence of cervical cancer, a disease associated with HPV.[11]

Studies show that people using latex condoms *correctly and consistently* during vaginal sex can reduce their risk of HIV by 85 percent. The risk for gonorrhea, chlamydia, and trichomoniasis can also be reduced.

Talking with a partner about condoms before having sex is a good idea. Some people are uncomfortable with the topic, but a little embarrassment is easier to get over than an STD. If a partner feels that a condom will interfere with sexual pleasure, knowing about condoms will help you explain the need for them. If a partner still refuses to use a condom, it may be time to say goodbye.

A BRIEF HISTORY OF CONDOMS

People have used condoms for thousands of years. The ancient Romans made them out of goats' bladders, the Chinese used oiled silk paper, and the Japanese had leather and tortoiseshell sheaths. The name probably comes from the Latin word for "receptacle." Here are a few highlights.

1000 B.C.: Ancient Egyptians use a linen sheath to protect them from disease.

A.D. 100–200: Earliest condom use in Europe is depicted in scenes from cave paintings at Comparelles in France.

1500s: Gabrielle Fallopius promotes the use of linen sheaths to protect against syphilis.

1700s: Oldest known condoms, made of fish and animal intestines, date back to this time in England. A trade in handmade condoms thrives in London.

1844: Charles Goodyear patents the vulcanization of rubber and begins mass producing condoms, soon known as "rubbers."

1880s: Julius Schmid makes condoms from sausage casings.

1919: Frederick Killian invents the latex condom.

1993: The Food and Drug Administration (FDA) approves the first female condom in the United States.

Choosing a condom: Not all condoms are for protection. Some are intended for sexual stimulation. Latex condoms are the only ones proven to prevent the transmission of STDs. Read the label carefully to make sure the condom is intended to prevent disease.

What Is a Female Condom?

A female condom is a thin sheath that is inserted into the vagina to protect against pregnancy and STDs. It is made from plastic or polyurethane and has been available in the United States since 1994.

A female condom looks like a pouch with a flexible ring at each end. Putting it on is a lot like inserting a tampon. The ring at the closed end is inserted into the vagina and fits around the cervix. The ring at the open end lies outside the vagina. It has a double purpose. It keeps the pouch from bunching up inside the vagina and guides the penis during penetration. It may also have a third advantage. It helps to cover areas outside the vagina that are susceptible to STDs transmitted skin-to-skin, such as herpes and genital warts. But this has not been proven yet.[12]

Like a male condom, a female condom should be removed carefully after intercourse. Also, it should only be used once. If a condom slips or gets twisted, pull it out and insert a new one. Lubricants can help. The female condom is not made from latex, so both oil-based and water-based lubricants are okay.

How does a female condom compare to a male condom for protection? No one really knows yet. Early studies show it protects well against HIV and probably prevents other STDs. One problem is that it seems to fail more often as a contraceptive than a male condom. It could be that women are just not experienced enough in using it.[13] Despite their drawbacks, female condoms offer women an alternative way to avoid STDs.

HOW REAL PEOPLE DEAL: HPV & CERVICAL CANCER

Alysa was known for having her act together. The popular college junior got good marks and was a leader in campus activities. When she and her boyfriend Seth decided to take their relationship to the next level, they were tested for STDs—and were relieved to discover they both were uninfected.

Alysa and Seth dated for several months; then they had a disagreement and broke up. A few months later, they got back together. Things were going great until Alysa went for her yearly PAP test and the doctor said she had changes in her cervix that might signal cancer. (The PAP test for cervical cancer is named for the researcher who developed it, Dr. George Papanicolaou.)

"I was really confused," she says. She remembered she'd seen her gynecologist every year since she was seventeen and her PAPs had always been normal.

Alysa was even more confused when the doctor told her she had HPV, the virus that causes genital warts and is the leading cause of cervical cancer. She had not had one symptom, and neither had Seth. But something was obviously wrong.

The HPV virus is shown above in a color-enhanced rendition based on a scanning electron microscope photo.

When Alysa told Seth about her diagnosis, he blamed himself because he had sex with someone else after he and Alysa broke up. But after talking to her doctor, Alysa realized that they would never be sure who had the virus first, because there is no test for HPV in people who do not have symptoms.

After three more PAP tests came back abnormal, the doctor performed a colposcopy, examining the cervix with a magnifying instrument. The test confirmed that Alysa had many cancerous cells. The doctor performed a loop electrosurgical excision procedure, which uses electrical current to remove cancerous cells.

Seth was with Alysa through the entire ordeal. She has now had several normal PAP tests and is cancer free. "It brought us closer together. We've been through so much stuff," Alysa says.

Her advice? "If you're going to have sex, get tested for STDs every six months. And young girls should get the shot for HPV," as recommended by the National Social Health Association.[14]

A condom with a spermicide (sperm-killer) containing nonoxynol-9 (N-9) may prevent pregnancy, but it will not reduce the risk of HIV or other STDs. In fact, N-9 can irritate the vagina or rectum, actually increasing the risk. Lubricants (substances that reduce friction), however, are a good idea. They can keep a condom from tearing and prevent irritation. Some condoms already come lubricated. Never use a separate oil-based lubricant, such as petroleum jelly, cold cream, hand lotion, or baby oil. They can weaken a latex condom and cause it to break more easily.

Buying a condom at a vending machine is okay as long as the condom is latex and labeled for disease prevention. Watch out for extreme temperature and direct sunlight exposure. And never use a condom if the expiration date has passed.

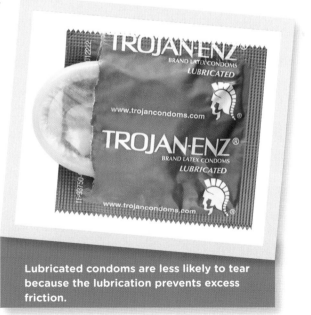

Lubricated condoms are less likely to tear because the lubrication prevents excess friction.

Using a condom: Always store condoms in a cool, dry place. Try not to carry one around for longer than a few hours. Avoid sunlight and extreme heat. A few hours of baking in a car's glove compartment can make a latex condom brittle, tacky, and unusable.

Older People Don't Get STDs

Everyone knows that people in their "golden years" do not have sex, so they never have to worry about STDs, right? Wrong! Maybe that was true in the past, but today people are living longer and having sex into their eighties and beyond. Many are divorced or widowed and dating again for the first time in years.

The facts speak for themselves. The CDC reported that twenty-four percent of people with HIV or AIDS in 2005 were age fifty and older. It was only seventeen percent in 2001. The increase is thanks partly to improved treatment, which allows people to live longer. But the over-fifty crowd also makes up fifteen percent of *new* HIV or AIDS diagnoses.[15] In one HIV study on older adults, over 60 percent of the group had been infected through heterosexual sex.[16]

Information about other STDs in older people is limited. As long as they are having unprotected sex, however, they are in just as much danger as anyone else.

As people live longer and stay sexually active, STDs are on the rise among individuals over the age of fifty.

Be careful removing a condom from the packet. Using teeth to open it can make holes in the condom. Check for defects like tears and holes in the tip. If the condom is brittle or sticks to itself, throw it away. Never use a damaged condom.

Use a brand-new condom for every sex act (vaginal, oral, or anal). Put it on as soon as there is an erection and *before* any sexual contact. The foreskin on an uncircumcised penis should be pulled back first. Start by pinching the tip of the condom to press air out. Then unroll the condom onto the penis (with the rim on the outside) all the way to its base. Leave room in the tip for semen to collect, check for trapped air, and make sure the outside is well-lubricated. (Air bubbles and dryness can cause a condom to break or tear.) After ejaculating, remove the condom right away, holding the rim to keep the semen from spilling and the condom from sliding off. Used condoms should be wrapped in a tissue and thrown in the trash.

Use a brand-new condom for every sex act (vaginal, oral, or anal). Put it on as soon as there is an erection and *before* any sexual contact.

A few words of warning: If a condom goes on incorrectly, start over again with a new one; if a condom breaks during sex, stop at once and start over again with a new one; *never* reuse a condom.

Birth Control Pills Protect Against STDs

Fiction! Birth control pills protect against pregnancy, not STDs. Although they are not 100 percent effective, condoms are the only contraceptive that can help protect against STDs.

OTHER WAYS TO REDUCE RISK

The following additional practices can reduce STD risk.

Limiting sexual partners. Choosing one partner who has sex only with you is called mutual monogamy. Both partners still need to get tested though, because either could have been infected by a previous partner and not know it. Some people believe that "serial monogamy"—having sex with one person at a time, even if just for a few weeks—is safe. This practice will not protect someone from STDs.

Avoiding drugs and alcohol. They impair good judgment, something people need to have when considering sex. Drugs and alcohol can make people feel aroused, but watch out. They also can make it difficult for a guy to have an erection! If someone is feeling so anxious about having sex that he or she needs drugs or alcohol to relax, maybe that person should wait. Responsible—and enjoyable—sex requires a clear head.

Communicating. People need to talk with partners about STDs, past sex partners, condoms, and getting tested. Young people should also communicate with their friends and parents. Being able to discuss sex and ask questions freely results in lower rates of STDs. A 2008 study of 200 college undergraduates found that students whose fathers were "in the loop" were less likely to do drugs or engage in risky sexual behavior. Students who were close to their moms were less likely to be involved in drugs, alcohol, and risky sexual activity.[17]

Getting educated about STDs. Besides reading this book, look for other information about sexual health, STDs, protection, and prevention. Learn about the different STDs, their symptoms, and how they spread. Check out condom use and other ways to reduce risk. Find out how to be tested and treated for the different STDs. Then educate everyone else—friends, family, and especially partners.

Getting tested for STDs. Chlamydia screening is recommended for all sexually active women from ages fifteen to twenty-four, whether or not they have symptoms.[18] Many young women believe that doctors routinely test for it. In 2003, however, only 30 percent of women under twenty-five with commercial health care plans were screened for chlamydia.[19] A national survey of U.S. physicians found that fewer than one-third were screening patients for STDs on a regular basis.[20]

Getting vaccinated against STDs. Newborns and children are now being given a vaccine to prevent hepatitis B as part of their immunization schedule. It is also recommended for sexually active adults. People involved in both oral and anal sex should also consider a vaccine against hepatitis A. Since 2006, a new HPV vaccine called Gardisil has been available. It protects against four HPV types that together cause seventy percent of cervical cancers and 90 percent of genital warts. The vaccine is given in three shots over six months to girls and women from ages nine to twenty-six.[21]

Getting treated for STDs. Someone diagnosed with an STD should take advantage of the treatments available. Many STDs are curable, and others can be managed. Getting treated will help prevent STDs from being passed on to others. People with STDs also have a responsibility to let their partners know so they can be tested, too.

Testing and Treatment

J ust about anyone who is or was sexually active is at risk of getting an STD. To paraphrase former U.S. Surgeon General C. Everett Koop, M.D., you never have sex with just one person, you have sex with everyone that person has slept with for the last ten years and everyone their partners have slept with.[1] So, in a way, a person can have what amounts to dozens, even hundreds, of sex partners in their lifetime without "sleeping around."

WHO SHOULD GET TESTED?

The CDC recommends that these people be tested for the following STDs:

- Sexually active women twenty-five years old and younger (chlamydia test every year)
- Sexually active people not in a long-term, mutually monogamous relationship (hepatitis B vaccination, yearly HIV test, chlamydia test if recommended by doctor)
- All men who have sex with men (hepatitis A and B vaccinations)
- Men who have sex with men who are not in a long-term, mutually monogamous relationship (hepatitis A and B vaccinations; HIV, syphilis, chlamydia, and gonorrhea tests at least once a year)
- Pregnant women (chlamydia, syphilis, HIV, hepatitis B tests at first visit to doctor for pregnancy or as early as possible; hepatitis C and gonorrhea tests if recommended by doctor)

- Anyone with or without symptoms who is seeking STD evaluation or treatment (hepatitis B vaccination; tests for syphilis, gonorrhea, and chlamydia if recommended by doctor).[2]

Suppose a person asks to be tested for "everything?" This is called a full STD screen, but it does not always include testing for HIV, herpes, or HPV, so people need to specifically request these tests from their doctors. The important point is that sexually active people *must* get tested, even if they use condoms or other barrier methods. Why? Because barrier methods are not hundred percent foolproof. Condoms can break, are often used incorrectly, and do not cover all areas of infection.

Vaccinations can prevent some STDs, such as hepatitis A and B.

People who do not realize they have STDs risk spreading them to all their future sex partners, and on and on, just as Dr. Koop warned. Sexually transmitted diseases can cause infertility, birth defects in babies, cancer, and even death. Thanks to the news media and Internet health sites, Americans know a lot about cancer, high cholesterol, obesity, and other health issues. So it is time for more people to learn more about STDs and sexual health.

FINDING THE RIGHT DOCTOR

If you feel comfortable discussing STDs with your family doctor, go to him or her. If you don't, one way to find a doctor or clinic with expertise in STDs is by checking the yellow pages under "sexually transmitted diseases" or "STD clinics," or by doing an Internet search. One organization, Planned Parenthood, has at least 860 centers throughout the country. More than 3 million STD tests and treatments are provided to men, women, and teens by Planned Parenthood every year.[3] People can also call a national STD hotline, such as the CDC's STDs Hotline, for information on clinics in their area (see "For More Information" in the back of this book). Many of these clinics are less expensive than regular doctors' offices or even free.

One caution: Doctors and other health care providers should not make patients feel guilty or ashamed, judge them, or try to inflict their religious or moral beliefs on them. Find another doctor if this happens.

THE MEDICAL HISTORY AND PHYSICAL EXAM

Most doctors do not test for STDs during a routine yearly exam unless a patient asks them to. Patients must be honest with their doctors about their sexual practices and any STD symptoms they are having. The doctor will start by asking questions and then perform an examination. Then the doctor will perform more complicated tests if he feels it is necessary.

The first part of any examination is called the medical history. The doctor asks what problem prompted the patient's visit and then asks questions to gather more information. Talking about STDs or other sexual concerns is embarrassing, but honesty is important. Patients should make sure the doctor knows about their sexual orientation because some STDs are more common among gay men. Doctors might assume patients are heterosexual if they do not say otherwise.

Next, the doctor performs a physical exam to look for signs of STDs. He concentrates on the genital, anal, and buttock areas, looking for sores, warts, redness, rashes, and other problems. He also checks the overall skin for rashes and examines the mouth and throat. He uses a long cotton swab to wipe areas that might be infected with STDs, collecting specimens of body fluids and discharge from sores. Then he sends the specimens to a laboratory where the bacteria, viruses, or other organisms are cultured (grown) and then examined under a microscope. Sometimes, he takes a biopsy (removes a small piece of skin) to be examined.

How They Work: Getting a Pelvic Examination

During a pelvic examination, the doctor checks a woman's internal and external reproductive organs for signs of disease. This exam is performed routinely on women over age twenty-one, whether they are sexually active or not. Most women go to a specialist called a gynecologist to have it done, and a PAP test may be performed at the same time. A PAP test involves scraping tissue from the cervix to check for early signs of cancer.

For this exam, the patient undresses from the waist down, covers her lower body with a paper drape, and lies on her back on an examination table. She puts her feet in stirrups and slides her buttocks to the end of the table, causing her legs to open wide. The doctor sits facing the patient at the end of the table and shines a bright light on the patient's genital area. Then she lubricates an instrument called a speculum and gently inserts it into the patient's vagina. Once the speculum is inserted all the way, the doctor opens the speculum to spread the vaginal walls so she can see the cervix at the opening of the uterus. Patients may feel a slight cramping, similar to menstrual cramps. The doctor examines the vaginal walls and cervix for signs of infection or other problems. If she sees any discharge, sores, warts, or other signs of STDs, she takes a swab to send to the lab for testing. To perform a PAP test, she uses a tiny brush and miniature plastic spatula to collect and remove a few cells from inside the cervix and around it. She rubs the cells on a glass slide or places them in a liquid and then sends them to a lab.

Gynecologists are specialists in the female reproductive system and frequently perform Pap tests.

Continued from previous page

Many women think the PAP test checks for STDs, but it does not. It only tests for cervical cancer. Patients who want to be tested for STDs should ask their doctor to also take vaginal and cervical samples to send to the lab. Otherwise, a doctor usually will not check for STDs unless she sees something suspicious.

After an external exam, the doctor performs a pelvic exam (an exam of a woman's internal reproductive organs). This allows the doctor to see the inside of the vagina and take specimens from there and the cervix. On a man he gently opens the urethra to check for discharge from the

How They Work: Getting a Urethral Swab

In men, a urethral swab is used to collect specimens from inside the penis to test for gonorrhea and chlamydia. The patient should not urinate for at least one hour before the test. During the test, he either lies on his back on an examination table or stands. The doctor cleans the end of the penis with sterile gauze or a cotton swab, and then gently inserts a thin swab (a stick with a cotton bud at the end) into the urethra. The swab is about an inch long. Once the swab is inserted, the doctor gently turns it making sure it comes into contact with all urethral surfaces. He leaves it in place for several seconds before withdrawing it. He then inserts the swab into a special container and sends it to the lab for culturing. Some labs can perform both gonorrhea and chlamydia tests on one specimen, while others require two specimens on two different swabs. Most men find this test uncomfortable, but luckily, it is over within a few seconds.

penis, and then swabs the area and sends the specimen to the lab for analysis.

If the patient has diarrhea, the doctor may take a stool specimen from the inside of the rectum to test for intestinal infections. He may also insert a small plastic instrument called a speculum into the rectum to check for changes in the rectal lining or warts and other skin problems. This procedure is called an anoscopy.

The doctor will also have blood drawn from the patient's arm to check for some STDs, such as syphilis, herpes, hepatitis, and HIV. This is usually done by a technician in the doctor's office or a diagnostic laboratory. The patient will also be asked to provide a urine sample, which will also be tested for evidence of STDs.

After the exam, the doctor will discuss his initial findings and give the patient time to ask questions. A definite diagnosis may not be possible until the blood and urine test results come back. If an STD can be diagnosed immediately, the doctor will discuss treatments and prescribe medication, if necessary. He may also tell the patient to come back for follow-up visits. The doctor will emphasize that the patient's partner or partners should also be tested and tell the patient not to have sexual contact with anyone until the test results come back.

After the exam, the doctor will discuss his initial findings and give the patient time to ask questions. A definite diagnosis may not be possible until the blood and urine test results come back.

The Doctor Notifies Patients' Sex Partners about STDs

This is mostly fiction. In 2002, researchers from the Division of STD Prevention at the CDC surveyed 7,300 U.S. doctors and found that 82 percent to 89 percent instructed patients newly diagnosed with an STD to notify sex partners themselves.[4]

Notifying sex partners might be the hardest thing a person ever has to do, but it must be done or the infection will be passed on. The doctor will tell the patient how far back to go to inform previous partners. Here are some suggestions to make talking to partners easier:

- Whether talking face to face or over the phone, pick a quiet place where you will not be disturbed.
- Try to stay calm as you break the news.
- Explain the doctor's diagnosis and the recommended treatment for everyone exposed.
- Explain that people without symptoms can still be infected.
- Try not to blame the other person for the STD. Some infections lie dormant for years.
- Be prepared for a negative reaction, even if the STD is easily treatable with antibiotics. Give them time to adjust.

One alternative to facing a partner alone is visiting the doctor together so he can explain the diagnosis and treatment options. Another alternative is third party partner notification. Public health clinics and state departments of health will often notify sex partners without giving the person's name. There are also Web sites where people with STDs can send anonymous cards to all their partners telling them they have been exposed to an STD.

TESTING FOR STDs

A full STD screen checks for as many as seventeen different infections. The following tests are used to diagnose each STD covered in this book.

Chlamydia

Several tests are used to diagnose chlamydia, but the nucleic acid amplification test (NAAT) is the most accurate. It checks for the genetic material (DNA) of the chlamydia bacterium in a urine sample. If infection is suspected in the throat or anal area, the doctor will take a specimen and have a culture done instead. During a culture, a small sample of an organism is grown in a laboratory to help diagnose the cause of an infection.

Gonorrhea

Testing involves taking swabs from the urethra and cervix in women, the urethra in men, and sometimes from the throat and anal area. Bacteria can often be seen under the microscope right away; if not, a culture will need to be done, which takes forty-eight hours to grow. A new test, nucleic acid hybridization, detects DNA in gonorrhea bacterium in urine or in swabs from infected areas. The NAAT is also used to diagnose gonorrhea.

Hepatitis B

Several blood tests are used to diagnose hepatitis B. The tests detect antigens (the virus itself, a foreign substance in the body) or antibodies (proteins the body makes to try to fight off the virus). Not all tests are done on every patient, but two or three tests may be done. The tests can tell a person's viral status: Do they have a new infection? Are they carriers? Have they recovered from an old infection? Have they been vaccinated against the virus? People who are newly infected may still test negative and may need to be tested again at a later date.

Herpes

Herpes can be tricky to diagnose because sores can resemble herpes and actually be from other causes. Even if a person has herpes, cultures show no virus about half the time.[5] The preferred test is to culture sores as soon as possible after

HOW REAL PEOPLE DEAL: HEPATITIS B

People donate blood so they can save someone else's life, but they never dream they could learn important information about their own health. In 1999, Tony Ngo, age forty-two, gave blood at his local blood bank in Orange County, California. A few weeks later he got a letter saying his blood was rejected because he was infected with hepatitis B.

Tony was shocked. He had no idea how he got the infection. He felt fine, so he didn't seek treatment, but the virus was silently damaging his liver. During the next two years, it destroyed his liver cells, leaving them so scarred they stopped functioning properly. While he waited for a liver transplant, he got sicker and sicker. None of his nine siblings were able to donate because they all had hepatitis B, too.

"I thought, 'I'm going to die,' " Tony said.

Hepatitis B was an epidemic in the Vietnamese-American community where Tony lived.[6] Some researchers think that this might be due to crowded living conditions and poverty in Vietnam, where the adults grew up, many while the Vietnam War was raging in the late 1960s. Most children born in the United States after 1990 have been vaccinated against the infection, but most older people have not. Around the country, one in eight Vietnamese-Americans has the disease, mainly adults.[7]

Tony was planning his funeral when a liver match was found. Today he sports a big scar on his abdomen and takes medicine every day to keep his body from rejecting the liver.

Many people in Tony's community are afraid to get tested for hepatitis B because they think people will shun them if they are infected. Tony dispels myths and helps them get tested. It is his way of saying thank you for being given a new lease on life.[8]

they appear. Results take seven to ten days. Blood tests are not commonly used because they are not accurate.

HIV

Because HIV infection is incurable and eventually turns into AIDS, a deadly disease, the hardest part of HIV testing is finding the courage to have it done. The virus is detectable in the blood of most people within three months of exposure, but it occasionally takes up to six months.

Tests are used to detect HIV and to check on the health of an infected person. The enzyme immunoassay test is done first, using a specimen of blood or saliva. This test is not hundred percent accurate, so a Western blot test or a test called immunofluorescence assay is done to verify the results. Both of these tests measure the amount of HIV antibodies in blood.

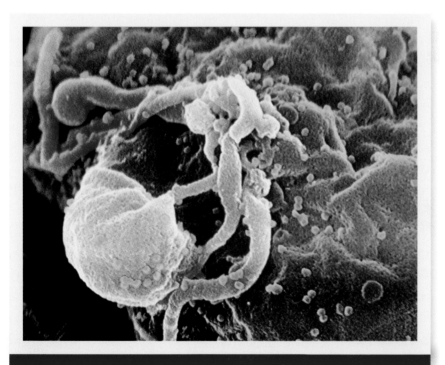

This electron microscope photograph shows the HIV virus (green) and a lymph cell (pink). The virus is detectable in the blood of most people within three hours of exposure.

Once HIV has been diagnosed, tests are performed to see how a person is doing. Cells in the immune system, called CD4 cells and helper T cells, can be measured by a blood test. These cells are the ones destroyed by HIV. If the cell counts (number of cells) are low, a person's immune system may need a boost with higher dosages of drugs or different drugs. Viral load tests measure the amount of virus in the blood and are also used to assess how well a person is doing.

A CDC biologist conducts a test in a Biological Safety Cabinet (BSC) in order to validate a rapid HIV test.

HPV

There is no test to detect HPV in men or women who do not have genital warts. People can actually fight off the virus on their own, or the virus can lie dormant in the body and cause symptoms later. Because HPV can occasionally cause cervical cancer, women should have a test called a PAP smear done yearly to check for early signs of this cancer. This test involves scraping the cervix and sending tissue samples to a lab to be examined.

A new test called the Hybrid Capture 2 HPV DNA test takes samples from the cervix and can tell if a woman is infected with the HPV virus that causes warts even if she has no visible symptoms. However, this test is only done to clarify an abnormal PAP test. It does not diagnose HPV in people without symptoms.

If a person has genital warts, an experienced doctor can usually diagnose HPV just by looking. To check for warts on the cervix, he may perform a colposcopy, in which a magnifying scope is used to see inside the vagina. Removing suspicious skin growths by freezing them with liquid nitrogen can also help diagnose their cause. Warts from HPV stay white and frozen longer than the normal skin around them, so if no white areas persist on a growth after freezing, that growth is not from HPV.

There is no test to detect HPV in men or women who do not have genital warts. People can actually fight off the virus on their own, or the virus can lie dormant in the body and cause symptoms later.

Pubic Lice and Scabies

The doctor can usually diagnose pubic lice just by looking at the infected areas. Lice can also be examined under a microscope.

Scabies may be confused with other skin rashes, so the best way to diagnose this infection is by scraping the skin bumps and looking under the microscope for the mites themselves or their waste products.

Syphilis

Two types of tests are used to diagnose syphilis: blood tests to detect antibodies and swabs taken from chancres to detect the syphilis bacterium. Most clinics do not have the special microscope necessary to perform this test, so blood tests are usually used for diagnosis. The most common ones are called the Venereal Disease Research Laboratory test and the Rapid Plasma Reagin test. If a person has a positive result from either of these tests, a second test called the Fluorescent

Blood tests are used to detect diseases including syphilis.

What Is a Culture?

Cultures are laboratory tests that are performed to discover which microorganisms are responsible for infections. When testing for STDs or other infections, tissue or body fluid specimens are placed in a substance called a medium that encourages their growth. Bacterial cultures are performed by spreading the specimen on several culture plates and then putting them in a container called an incubator at body temperature for one to two days. Any bacteria that were present will multiply and be visible under a microscope. They can then be identified. Viral cultures are grown by mixing the specimen in a test tube with commercially prepared animal cells. If a virus is present, it causes the animal cells to change in certain ways that can be seen under a microscope. Some viruses take several days or even several weeks to grow.

A CDC researcher closely inspects a Petri dish filled with agar, a culture medium, which has been inoculated with a specimen. The researcher will then determine what kind of microorganism is present.

Treponemal Antibody Absorbed test is done. The bacteria may take up to three months after infection to appear in the blood, although most people test positive within a few weeks.

Trichomoniasis

To diagnose this parasite in women, the doctor does a pelvic examination to look for signs of the infection and to get a sample of the vaginal discharge to view under the microscope. The classic sign is called "strawberry cervix"—a red, irritated cervix covered with small red dots. He then examines the vaginal discharge under a microscope in his office. This is the most common way to diagnose trichomoniasis, but it is not the most accurate. Up to 40 percent of cases are missed during a typical examination.[9] For this reason, the doctor may decide to send a sample of the vaginal secretion to a lab to be cultured, a much more accurate test.

Men may be tested by taking cultures from their urine, semen, or urethra, but these tests are not very accurate. Most men have no symptoms and only consult a doctor after they find out a female sexual partner has trichomoniasis.

Be sure to complete your entire prescribed course of drug treatment for any STD, even if you're feeling better or your symptoms go away.

TREATMENTS FOR STDs

Treatment for STDs varies according to the type of infection. Bacterial STDs are curable with medication; so are those caused by protozoa and parasites. So far, no cures have been found for viral STDs, but treatments—from medicine to minor surgery—can ease the symptoms and allow people to lead relatively normal lives.

No matter what STD a person is being treated for, they should follow these general guidelines:

- Take all the medicine the doctor prescribes, even if the symptoms go away.
- Do not resume having sex, even with protection, until the doctor says it is okay.
- Notify all current and past sex partners about the infection so they can get treated, too. The doctor will tell the patient how far back he should go.
- Be prepared to have a repeat test to be sure the infection is gone. This is especially important for pregnant patients.

CURING BACTERIAL STDs

The bacterial STDs chlamydia, gonorrhea, and syphilis are easy to cure if they are discovered early. However, they are also easy to catch again, so sexually active people may need to be tested on a regular basis.

Chlamydia: Oral antibiotics (pills) are the treatment. The drugs most often used to eradicate chlamydia are doxycycline and azithromycin. People who are allergic to these drugs can take erythromycin, ofloxacin, or levofloxacin instead. Erythromycin is given to pregnant women with chlamydia because the other drugs can harm the unborn baby.

Gonorrhea: Antibiotics are also used to treat genital and anal gonorrhea. Cefriaxone is given as a shot, and ciprofloxacin, levofloxacin, and ofloxacin are given in pill form. Unfortunately, these last three drugs are becoming less effective in treating gonorrhea in many parts of the world, including the United States, because the bacteria are becoming resistant.

Antibiotics must be taken for a longer time if gonorrhea has caused PID or epididymitis. Gonorrhea that infects the eyes must be treated by an eye doctor. If the infection has spread to other organs, such as the joints or heart, hospitalization and treatment with intravenous (into a vein) antibiotics is necessary.

Syphilis: The treatment for syphilis is penicillin—one of the first antibiotics invented. It is always given as a shot, and one dose usually gets rid of primary, secondary, and early latent stage syphilis. Because the dose is so high and the bacteria are killed off so quickly, some people get chills, headache, muscle aches, and fever about eight hours after the shot. The rash or chancres may even get worse temporarily. This is called the Jarisch-Herxheimer reaction and usually goes away in twenty-four hours. People with late-stage latent syphilis and those who do not know how long they have been infected need penicillin shots every week for three weeks.

Other antibiotics, such as doxycycline or tetracycline, are used for people with primary or secondary syphilis who have penicillin allergies. However, experts and drug manufacturers advise that it may not be safe to give these drugs to children and teens because they can cause staining of developing teeth.[10, 11] Penicillin is the only safe antibiotic for pregnant women.

TREATING VIRAL STDs

Because they do not respond to antibiotics, viral STDs can be complicated to treat. Experts continue to search for more effective, longer lasting treatments, as well as cures.

Hepatitis B: People who were exposed recently to hepatitis B should see their doctors immediately and get a shot of hepatitis B immunoglobulin and the first of three shots of hepatitis B vaccine. People who had sex with someone who has or might have hepatitis B, who shared needles during drug use, or who were accidentally stuck with a needle (such as nurses and other healthcare workers) fall into this category.

People who have symptoms of hepatitis B (such as extreme fatigue, yellow skin, and vomiting) usually get better by resting, eating right, drinking plenty of fluids, and avoiding alcohol and drugs that can harm the liver for at least three to four months. People with severe infections, other medical problems, or those over age forty may need to be hospitalized.

Those who have had hepatitis B for a long time (chronic hepatitis) must take drugs to stop liver damage. Drugs include interferon, lamivudine, adefovir, dipivoxil, and entecavir. Researchers are exploring other drugs and treatments. All people with hepatitis B should get a shot to protect them against hepatitis A.

Herpes: Antiviral drugs are used to prevent outbreaks (sores), to lessen symptoms, and reduce the chance of passing the virus on to partners. This is called suppressive therapy.

Many of these drugs are effective for both type 1 and type 2 herpes, although they do not kill the virus.

Pills to prevent outbreaks are acyclovir, valacyclovir, and famciclovir. They are for people who already have the virus and will not keep someone from catching it. They stop the virus from multiplying so people either stop having outbreaks or have them less often and less severely. People who have a first outbreak usually take one of these drugs for ten days; then they use the drug every time they have an outbreak or feel like they are about to have one (called intermittent treatment). People who have frequent outbreaks may take the drug every day. This reduces the number of outbreaks in 70 to 80 percent of people and completely prevents them in about 50 percent.[12]

Creams to rub on the skin are also available, but they are not very effective against genital herpes. However, a prescription penciclovir cream has been successful in treating cold sores (oral herpes) and nonprescription docasanol cream is also effective.

HIV: Today, people infected with HIV are living many more years by taking drugs that slow down the virus's replication in the body and keep it from developing into AIDS. People take the drugs every day for the rest of their lives. Taking several drugs at once (combination therapy) works the best.

Five types of antiviral drugs are currently on the market, and each works in a different way to ward off AIDS. Two new types of drugs are fusion inhibitors and integrase inhibitors. Fusion inhibitors keep HIV from getting into healthy cells of the immune system and infecting them. Integrase inhibitors cripple integrase, an enzyme HIV needs to get into cells.

Practicing safer sex is especially important for people infected with HIV, and not just because they could pass the infection on to others. Because their immune systems are fragile, people with HIV are more apt to catch other STDs and get more severe cases.

Viral load tests and CD4 and T-helper cell counts are not treatments, but they are used to monitor how well drug treatments are working. Blood tests are done every three to six months to check these counts. Drug therapy is successful if the viral load is at levels that are untraceable.

Practicing safer sex is especially important for people infected with HIV, and not just because they could pass the infection on to others. Because their immune systems are fragile, people with HIV are more apt to catch other STDs and get more severe cases.

People with HIV also need to take drugs to prevent opportunistic infections—serious illnesses that they are more susceptible to. Some of these illnesses are a type of pneumonia called *Pneumocystis carinii*, tuberculosis, and genital herpes. Different drugs are used to treat each opportunistic infection.

HPV: No treatment exists for the virus itself, but there are treatments for genital warts, the main symptom of HPV. Sometimes, warts go away on their own. If they do not, they can be removed by cyrotherapy (freezing with liquid nitrogen), electrosurgery (cutting out with an electrified blade or wire), regular surgery (cutting out with a scalpel), laser surgery (removing with a high-intensity beam of light), or medicine

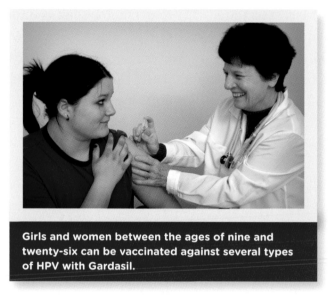

Girls and women between the ages of nine and twenty-six can be vaccinated against several types of HPV with Gardasil.

applied to the wart. Removing warts does not mean a person is no longer infectious, but it may reduce the chance of infecting others.

Gardasil is an HPV vaccine for girls and women ages nine to twenty-six. It prevents infection from the two types of HPV that cause 90 percent of genital warts (HPV 6 and 11) and two types that cause 70 percent of cervical cancers (HPV 16 and 18).[13]

Cervical cancer is a serious consequence of HPV. But the number of women with genital warts who end up with cervical cancer is very small, especially in view of the fact that 20 million people in this country are infected with HPV.[14] Cervical cancer can be cured if it is diagnosed and treated early, but a yearly PAP test can detect problems before cancer develops.

CURING PROTOZOAL AND PARASITIC STDs

Like bacterial STDs, protozoal and parasitic STDs are completely curable. The parasites pubic lice and scabies are the only STDs that can be diagnosed without lab tests. The doctor can tell by looking if a person has them.

Phthirus pubis is the scientific name for the pubic or crab louse. Normally, Phthirus pubis is transmitted from person to person through direct sexual contact, and thereafter, infests the widely spaced pubic hair region in adults, and the eyelashes in affected children.

Pubic lice: These parasites are treated with creams, lotions, or shampoos called pediculicides, the same medicines used to treat head lice. Some of these treatments are available at drugstores without a prescription. The medicine is applied to the infected area, left on for up to ten minutes, and then washed off. Afterward, the eggs can be removed from the hair shafts with the fingernails or a fine-tooth comb. These products can be used everywhere on the body except the eyebrows and eyelashes. Getting rid of lice in the eye area requires applying a prescription product similar to petroleum jelly to the brows and lashes twice a day for ten days.

Regular petroleum jelly is not recommended because it can cause eye irritation.

Anyone else in close contact with the infected person during the previous month should also be treated. All clothing and bedding the person was in contact with during the past seventy-two hours should be washed in hot water and dried in the dryer on the hot cycle.

Scabies: Treating scabies requires neck-to-toe application of an over-the-counter or prescription pediculicide. The medicine must be left on for eight to fourteen hours, so it should be applied before bed and washed off in the morning. An alternate treatment is taking a pill called ivermectin right after scabies are diagnosed by a doctor and then two weeks later. This drug is not recommended for young children or women who are pregnant or breastfeeding. Clothing and bedding should be washed in the same way as for pubic lice.

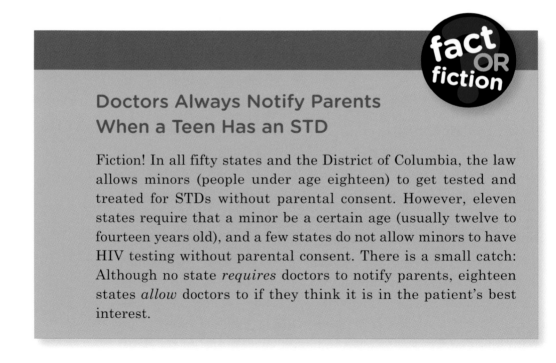

Doctors Always Notify Parents When a Teen Has an STD

Fiction! In all fifty states and the District of Columbia, the law allows minors (people under age eighteen) to get tested and treated for STDs without parental consent. However, eleven states require that a minor be a certain age (usually twelve to fourteen years old), and a few states do not allow minors to have HIV testing without parental consent. There is a small catch: Although no state *requires* doctors to notify parents, eighteen states *allow* doctors to if they think it is in the patient's best interest.

Trichomoniasis: This protozoal infection usually disappears after taking one of two antibiotics: metronidazole or tinidazole. Both men and women take the pill only once. If this does not work, the doctor will repeat the treatment or send the patient to a specialist if the infection still does not go away. Patients are warned not to drink alcohol for twenty-four hours after taking metronidazole and seventy-two hours after taking tinidazole. Drinking will cause violent nausea and vomiting.

Tinidazole is not recommended for pregnant women, but metronidazole is considered safe.

CHAPTER SIX

Outlook for the Future

"We've achieved important successes in recent years. . . but for the millions of people whose health remains at risk, our continued commitment to STD prevention is essential."[1] Those words were spoken by Kevin Fenton, M.D., director of the CDC's National Center for HIV/AIDS, Viral Hepatitis, STD, and TB Prevention. Is it possible to overcome the threat that STDs still are today? Dr. Fenton says yes.

One of the CDC's purposes is to encourage research, develop goals and policy, and support services that will meet the needs of individual communities. The agency works with education groups, state and local health departments, and national and community organizations in an effort to prevent STDs and their complications. What will the CDC bring us tomorrow? New treatments? Improved prevention programs? A vaccine for HIV? A cure for HPV or herpes?

ADVANCES IN PREVENTION

Sexually transmitted disease prevention is no easy task. It means changing the kinds of behaviors that get people infected. It also means making sure that people with STDs do not infect others. Everyone agrees that education is important. But how do you educate the people who need it the most? The CDC believes that outreach is the key.

According to the CDC, no single approach will work to reduce or eliminate STDs, so they have developed a five-part strategy to do the job.

The CDC's five-part plan includes several activities:

1. Educate people at risk to practice safer sexual behaviors.
2. Identify people with STDs who are not likely to look for diagnosis and treatment.
3. Effectively diagnose and treat people with STDs.
4. Find, evaluate, treat, and counsel the sex partners of people with STDs.
5. Vaccinate people at risk for preventable STDs before they are exposed to them.[2]

EDUCATION PROGRAMS

With so many people unaware of the dangers of STDs, education is an essential ingredient for prevention. And it does make a difference how young someone is. Over the past twenty years, sex education in schools has become more widespread in the United States and is now being taught at an earlier age. A recent study of young people proved that timing is everything. The adolescents in the study who had formal sex education before the first time they had sex were not as likely to engage in risky sex behavior or have sexual intercourse at an early age.[3]

A different way to teach people about STDs is through mass media campaigns. In one campaign, a public service announcement about STDs was televised for three months. Its target audience was young adults prone to risky sex behavior. The result? It increased their condom use by about thirteen percent.[4]

Educating people can also be done with a sense of humor. Another media campaign by a not-for-profit Internet group tried to promote sexual health in a fun way. The group held a contest to design men's and women's underwear—with messages written on them about preventing STDs and maintaining healthy relationships.

The CDC is encouraging people to educate each other about STDs by sending online greeting cards. The "Health-e-Cards" available on the CDC's Web site contain key facts and Web addresses to raise awareness of STDs or HIV testing.

INTERVENTION PROGRAMS

The CDC realizes that education alone is not always enough to motivate behavior change, especially for people at high risk. So they have developed a behavioral intervention approach that targets people who are difficult to reach.

One successful program called Project FIO (The Future Is Ours) is for heterosexual women living in areas of New York City where the risk for HIV is high. The interactive program holds eight two-hour sessions in family planning clinics. Sessions include group discussion, lectures, printed materials, and role playing. The women learn about their own personal risks for HIV and other STDs. They are also taught to identify barriers to safer sex and develop strategies to communicate better with male partners.[5]

Psychologists have discovered that behavioral intervention programs work for adolescents, too. Research shows that such programs delay the first time young people have intercourse *and* protect sexually active youth from STDs, including HIV. When they are combined with education programs, behavioral interventions also improve skills for negotiating lower-risk sex and increase how often young people talk about safer sex.[6]

In an effort to get the message out in a simpler way, the CDC has a twenty-three-minute HIV/STD intervention video called "Safe in the City," which is designed for waiting rooms in STD clinics. In a controlled trial, the video has proved to reduce new infections by ten percent in people who were exposed to it. Although the program was evaluated for adult clinic patients, an agency can determine if the content of the video and the prevention messages are appropriate for adolescent audiences. Anyone can order the DVD or download it to his or her computer, iPod, Sony Playstation, or cell phone.[7]

HOW REAL PEOPLE DEAL: EVEN THE HEALTH CONSCIOUS GET HERPES

Christin, age twenty-two, had always been health conscious. So before she and her new boyfriend Alec had sex, she insisted they both be tested for every STD in the book. She was relieved when both their results came back negative.

She and Alec dated for five months, and Christin assumed it was an exclusive relationship. Then one day she noticed some small red bumps on her outer labia. She thought they were ingrown hairs, but a few days later, they turned into painful open sores. "As I checked them out with a hand mirror, a chill went through me," Christin says. "I had a terrifying suspicion what might be causing them."

She wasted no time getting to the doctor. In the office, the doctor took a blood test and a skin test and explained that the results would be back in three days.

"The doctor looked so sad when she broke the news that I had herpes," Christin remembers. "I immediately burst into tears. After I left the office I ran to my car and sobbed so hard, a security guard knocked on the window and asked me if I was okay."

When Christin confronted Alec later, he admitted he had been having sex with another woman. Worse yet, he knew the other woman had herpes. Christin split with him on the spot.

Feeling isolated and betrayed, she crawled into bed and hid from the world for two days. Her first herpes outbreak lasted six weeks, and the sores were painful, then itchy as they healed.

Christin was open with her family and close friends about the infection, and that helped her get through the next few

Continued on next page

Continued from previous page

months. After she had two more outbreaks, the doctor gave her a new medicine that she takes daily. Now she only gets a brief outbreak about every four months. "Not having outbreaks so often helped me to calm down and start living again, and that included dating," she says.

"I'm always upfront about my disease on the first date," Christin says. "Surprisingly, most guys are understanding." After a year and a half, Christin says herpes barely affects her life anymore, except in one major, positive way. "I decided to go to nursing school so I can help other women become more proactive about their health," she says.[8]

The CDC's "Safe in the City" video has proved to reduce new STD infections by 10 percent in people who watched it.

Psychologists have discovered that behavioral intervention programs work for adolescents, too. Research shows that such programs delay the first time young people have intercourse *and* protect sexually active youth from STDs, including HIV.

The CDC considers intervention a priority for the future. The agency has a national network of core training programs for public health professionals working in STD/HIV prevention. The programs teach skills such as interviewing, problem solving, field investigation, partner notification and referral, and helping patients manage infections and prevent new ones.

DIAGNOSIS AND TREATMENT

The CDC works hard to make diagnosis and treatment of HIV and STDs easier. It made HIV-antibody testing more available in 2004 by supporting about 11,000 HIV-antibody test sites that performed 2.2 million tests for people at high risk. The tests were anonymous and confidential, and the sites offered counseling to all their clients. When people tested positive, they referred their partners for medical evaluation and testing.

People can also perform simpler screening for HIV and other STDs with rapid tests and tests that use oral fluids, urine, and blood from a fingerstick. The CDC now recommends testing

How They Work: Rapid or Point-of-Care Tests

Rapid tests, sometimes called "point-of-care" tests, are screening tests that can provide results in less than an hour in a doctor's office or clinic. The first rapid test was approved by the FDA in 2002 for HIV screening. The doctor takes blood from a vein or a finger, or uses a special device to collect oral fluids (fluids other than saliva), from the mouth to check for HIV antibodies. Rapid tests are as accurate as traditional screening tests, but a positive result still has to be confirmed with a follow-up test before making a diagnosis.

Rapid tests are also available for herpes and trichomoniasis screening. Progress is being made on a test for syphilis, but more work is needed for chlamydia and gonorrhea. Rapid tests can mean faster treatment and better prevention from transmitting infections.

HIV rapid tests during routine medical exams, at clinics, and in nontraditional settings.[9]

Home testing kits were first licensed in 1997, but the only two approved by the FDA for STDs are the Home Access HIV-1 Test System and Home Access Health's Hepatitis C Check. They are home collection kits that involve placing a few drops of blood from a pricked finger on a specially treated card. The card is then mailed to a licensed lab and customers get an ID number to use when calling for the results.[10, 11]

To remind people to be tested, there is National HIV Testing Day (NHTD), an annual campaign of the National Association of People with AIDS (NAPWA), which encourages people at risk to get voluntary HIV counseling and testing every year on June 27.

This rapid HIV test uses oral fluid (fluids other than saliva), to detect the virus. Rapid tests for STDs such as HIV are recommended during routine medical exams in some settings.

PARTNER SERVICES PROGRAMS

The CDC is always looking for new ways to improve partner notification and treatment. In October of 2008, the agency came out with guidelines for its newly integrated partner services programs. Partner services include all the services that should be offered to people with HIV or other STDs and their sexual or needle-sharing partners. The goal is to reduce the future rate of transmitting HIV or other STDs through early diagnosis, treatment, and prevention services for infected people.

Since people with HIV are often infected with another STD as well, it made no sense to offer them separate partner services programs. Instead the new recommendations encourage

STD, HIV, and other public health programs to work together to offer services that will benefit their clients the most.

Some principles of partner services are that they be client centered, confidential, voluntary, free, and available to everyone. The idea is to make them as comfortable and nonthreatening as possible. The primary steps in the process are (1) to identify people recently diagnosed with HIV or other STDs; (2) to contact those people to see if they have gotten their test results, been offered medical care, and received any medical services including treatment; (3) to discuss the need for those people to notify their partners and to offer partner services to help with notification; (4) if people agree to use partner services, to interview them about partners they had during the time they were exposed to HIV or another STD; (5) to try to contact any partners named and notify them of their exposure; and (6) to counsel located partners, referring them to testing, medical care, and other prevention services.

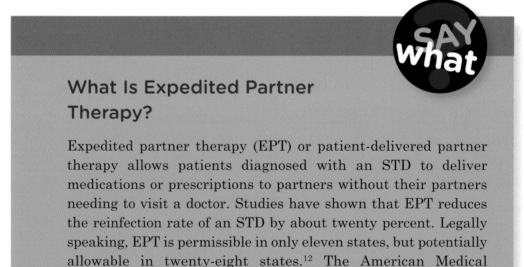

What Is Expedited Partner Therapy?

Expedited partner therapy (EPT) or patient-delivered partner therapy allows patients diagnosed with an STD to deliver medications or prescriptions to partners without their partners needing to visit a doctor. Studies have shown that EPT reduces the reinfection rate of an STD by about twenty percent. Legally speaking, EPT is permissible in only eleven states, but potentially allowable in twenty-eight states.[12] The American Medical Association recommends using EPT for gonorrhea and chlamydia infections in men and women only when other management strategies do not work.[13]

If an individual refuses to participate in partner services, other approaches can be offered, such as "expedited partner therapy."

THE INTERNET: A TOOL FOR PREVENTION

The Internet is a powerful tool for communication and consequently a powerful tool for STD and HIV prevention. Google "sexually transmitted diseases" and over five million results pop up. Try "HIV" and over seventy million appear. But the Internet is not just a source of education and information about STDs.

With the rise of chat rooms and sex sites on the Internet, people from high-risk groups are meeting online to arrange sexual encounters. AIDS organizations are beginning to use these sites for online interventions. Staff members log on to a chat room, creating a user name like "askemeaboutSTDs," and answer any appropriate questions that come their way.

The Internet is also a new medium for partner services. AIDS organizations use the term *Internet-based partner services* to refer to the process of using the Internet to notify a person of his or her exposure to an STD. People who engage in anonymous sex online may know only the e-mail addresses or screen names of their sex partners. As a result, the Internet may be the only way for health professionals to notify partners and provide the appropriate services.

VACCINES ON THE HORIZON

The CDC's final strategy is to vaccinate people at risk who have not been infected yet. Only a few STDs, however, can be prevented by vaccines. Those vaccines are for prevention of HPV infections and hepatitis A and B. Vaccines for other STDs, including HIV and the herpes viruses (known as Herpes Simplex Virus, or HSV) are either being developed or are undergoing clinical trials.

HSV Vaccine: One vaccine for HSV has already passed preliminary testing for safety and effectiveness. This clinical trial, called the *Herpevac Trial for Women*, is testing the vaccine in women who have not been infected with HSV, which causes cold sores and genital herpes. Earlier studies have shown that the vaccine was able to reduce the risk of infection in women who were not previously infected by about 75 percent. Unfortunately, the vaccine was ineffective in men and in women who were already infected with HSV 1.[14]

HPV Vaccine: Studies for an alternative vaccine for HPV called Cervarix™ are being conducted, but it has not yet been approved by the FDA. Unlike Gardasil, which protects against four HPV types, Cervarix™ targets two types—HPV 16 and 18. Like Gardasil, it is given in three doses over a six-month period.

What Are Clinical Trials?

Clinical trials are research studies that test the effectiveness and safety of new drugs, procedures, or medical devices on a group of people. The group may be divided in half, with half taking the new drug or following the procedure. The other half is the control group.

Clinical trials are frequently divided into phases or steps. Phase I is done with a small group of patients. It usually evaluates safety, determines a safe dosage, and identifies side effects. If Phase I is successful, then Phase II is repeated with a larger group to further evaluate the safety and effect of the treatment. Phase III trials are conducted with an even larger group and may be compared to current treatments. A Phase IV trial is conducted after the treatment is on the market and monitors its long-term effects.

Many STD or HIV drugs never make it to the market. Some even end with Phase I. A few, like Gardisil, actually get approved by the FDA to go on the market. These are the ones that go through Phase IV trials.

Neither vaccine gives complete protection from other HPV types, some of which can cause cervical cancer. That means women who have been vaccinated should still continue to undergo cervical cancer screening.

No one knows how long these vaccines will provide immunity against HPV. Studies are now being performed to decide if booster vaccinations will be necessary. Also, research is under way to determine if a vaccine can prevent infection with other HPV types.[15]

HIV Vaccines: Although there is no vaccine for HIV yet, researchers are studying three different types of vaccines that may prevent HIV infection. The strategy is to use the vaccines alone or in combination to enhance the body's overall immune response to HIV. The three types are:

- Subunit vaccines, which contain parts of the HIV virus made in a laboratory using genetic engineering. These man-made subunits can prompt an anti-HIV response in the body, but it may be too weak to last.
- Recombinant vector vaccines made from non HIV-viruses that are weakened or do not cause disease in humans. These vaccines carry copies of HIV genes into cells so that the body can produce HIV proteins to stimulate an anti-HIV response, which may be stronger.
- DNA vaccines that also introduce HIV genes into the body. With these vaccines, "naked" DNA is injected directly into the body. The cells then use it to produce HIV proteins to create an immune response.[16]

Clinical trials are research studies that test the effectiveness and safety of new drugs, procedures, or medical devices on a group of people.

ADVANCES IN TREATMENT

The irony is that treatments and cures already exist for many STDs. In fact, the CDC has been publishing *Guidelines* for treating STDs and HIV since 1982. Every four years, they update the *Guidelines*, using a scientific review process. They consult with outside experts who examine the most up-to-date information about STDs, and they update even further when a new drug, treatment, or intervention program becomes available.

The treatment of STDs can be complicated, however, especially when new viruses emerge the way HIV did in 1981. Other problems arise when a virus becomes resistant to a drug–which occurred in the early years of HIV and more recently with gonorrhea. As scientists continue to learn more about STDs, new treatments become possible. That is why there are so many clinical trials and studies being developed in the areas of STD and HIV research.

> The treatment of STDs can be complicated, especially when new viruses emerge the way HIV did in 1981. Other problems arise when a virus becomes resistant to a drug—which occurred in the early years of HIV and more recently with gonorrhea.

Gonorrhea Treatment: Drug-resistant gonorrhea has become a worldwide problem in recent years. Drugs that were once effective have been removed from the CDC's treatment guidelines because now gonorrhea bacteria exist that cannot be killed by those drugs. The only class of antibiotics still used for gonorrhea and its complications are the cephalosporins. The new recommended treatment for all gonorrhea infections is an injection of ceftriaxone. Cefixime, an oral drug, only recently became available in the United States.[17] Meanwhile, clinical studies are being performed in laboratories to determine the effectiveness of other antibiotics, especially oral drugs, against gonorrhea. The search for a new drug is a priority. If the cephalosporins lose their effectiveness, gonorrhea could become incurable.

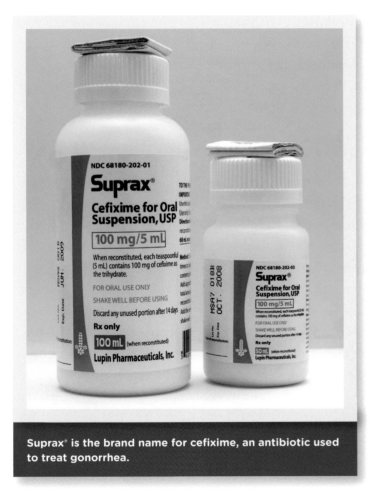

Suprax® is the brand name for cefixime, an antibiotic used to treat gonorrhea.

HIV Treatment: Besides developing vaccines to prevent HIV, researchers are working on therapeutic vaccines for people already infected with the virus. Therapeutic HIV vaccines are designed to boost the body's immune response to HIV so that the infection can be better controlled. If these vaccines work the way researchers hope they do, people in the future will not have to rely solely on the antiretroviral drugs they now use, which may cause serious side effects.

Therapeutic HIV vaccines are in the early stages of development in clinical trials and will not be available for several years—if they work at all. They will not be a cure, but they do offer hope for the future of HIV treatment.

Other Clinical Trials: The National Cancer Institute (NCI) is working with researchers on therapeutic HPV vaccines to prevent cancer in women who are already exposed to HPV. Also, new hepatitis B vaccines are being developed for infected people who respond poorly or not at all to the currently approved vaccines.

IMPACT OF HIV AND AIDS IN THE UNITED STATES

Sadly, more than half a million people have died from AIDS in the United States since it was first identified in 1981. Over a million people today are estimated to be living with HIV, a quarter of them unaware that they have the infection. Although the number of people dying from AIDS has dropped significantly, another 40,000 people are diagnosed with HIV every year.[18]

Today, HIV in the United States mostly affects racial and ethnic minorities and gay men. The virus is increasing among heterosexuals and women. Unfortunately, homophobia (fear of homosexuals, which can cause discrimination and make people reluctant to identify themselves as gay), poverty, unemployment, and lack of health care influence

HIV-risk behaviors and discourage people from getting tested and treated.

Progress is being made, though. The CDC has established disease-monitoring systems and is launching a national education and intervention effort, as was mentioned earlier in this chapter. It has also set up a National AIDS Hotline and a National AIDS Information Clearinghouse and updated its guidelines for prevention and treatment.

In December of 2008, the CDC revealed that the transmission rate of HIV had declined dramatically, a sign that prevention programs were beginning to work. But more needs to be done. Developing an HIV vaccine, expanding prevention programs, and finding other ways to reach out to people at risk are all an urgent priority.

HIV AND AIDS WORLDWIDE

The problem of HIV in the United States cannot compare to its impact in other parts of the world. The statistics are staggering. More than 25 million people worldwide have lost their lives to AIDS-related diseases. An estimated 2.1 million men, women, and children died as a result of AIDS in 2007. Another 33.2 million are living with HIV, most of whom will probably die over the next ten years.

More than 25 million people worldwide have lost their lives to AIDS-related diseases. An estimated 2.1 million men, women, and children died as a result of AIDS in 2007.

In Asia, the numbers are also high. In 2006, India was thought to have between 2 and 3 million people living with HIV. China's epidemic was estimated at 700,000 and Thailand's at 580,000. By the end of 2007, Latin America had 1.6 million people with HIV, while Eastern Europe/Central Asia more than doubled its 2001 infected population from 630,000 to 1.6 million.

Africa, with some of the poorest countries in the world, has been hardest hit by the virus. One fourth of Botswana's population is infected with HIV. In four other southern countries, one adult in five has the virus. And South Africa has more people with AIDS than any other country—5.5 million.[19]

Education, prevention programs, tests, and drugs are needed, especially in poor developing countries where access to knowledge and treatment is a challenge.

The global HIV problem is as complicated as the countries that suffer from it. It is affected by poverty, lack of education, poor health practices, and gender inequality. More money is being spent now on preventing new infections and treating the disease, but even more is needed. Education makes a difference, but not unless it reaches the people who need it. Prevention works, but not without access to the tools that make it possible. Medicine is available, but it is useless if it is not taken properly.

ISSUES FOR FUTURE WORLD TREATMENT PROGRAMS

Successful treatment programs require not just money. Effective programs must address these issues:

- HIV counseling and testing are the first step. People need to be encouraged to use these services, perhaps by including them in routine health care.
- People may need help in following treatment requirements, possibly requiring transportation or emotional support.

- Good nutrition is important, especially during treatment, so that people can stay healthy longer.
- Medications for other infections need to be available.
- Treatment centers need the basic facilities for testing, consulting, and securely storing medications.
- An uninterrupted supply of medication is necessary so people can continue their treatment on a daily basis.
- A sufficient number of health workers need to be recruited and trained.
- Patients should be monitored to be sure they are following their drug regimens.
- Mobile outreach services help make universal access to treatment possible.
- People may need to be convinced that treatment can save lives.

ORGANIZATIONS THAT PROVIDE SUPPORT

There are numerous organizations dedicated to supporting the countries of the world in their fight against HIV and AIDS.

The World Health Organization (WHO) plays a major role by providing technical support to its member states. Its goal is to make access to HIV and AIDS support universal. The organization works with other agencies in the health field to deliver HIV services, such as policy development, technical guidance, training for health workers, and a supply of HIV medicines. It also monitors the global spread of HIV/AIDS and the availability of treatment and prevention services, as well as advocating for more global attention to the disease. According to WHO, the number of new HIV infections around the globe has leveled off. Meanwhile, fewer people are dying of AIDS, and the antiretroviral therapy is allowing people to live longer with HIV. So even though the number of new infections is lower, the general HIV population continues to grow, providing new challenges.

Part of a WHO-supported effort, public health officials in Wuhan, China, promote safer sex through proper condom usage.

The International AIDS Society is an association of HIV/AIDS professionals who join together to present new research and share practices that advance the fight against the infection. The society is one of the major organizers of the International AIDS Conferences. At the 2008 Conference in Mexico City, participants discussed how to improve prevention efforts globally and called for continued support for an AIDS vaccine to end the pandemic.

The International AIDS Vaccine Initiative is a global partnership whose mission is to develop a safe, effective, accessible, preventive HIV vaccine that can be used worldwide. Since 2003, its network of partners have developed six possible vaccines and performed clinical trials in Asia, Africa, Europe, and North America.

The International HIV/AIDS Alliance is made up of organizations that support community action on AIDS in developing countries. They have already supported some of the poorest communities in over forty developing countries with HIV prevention, care, and access to treatment.

Dr. Fenton is right. It is possible to overcome the threat of HIV and STDs today. The tools are there. It is just a matter of learning how to use them.

The map on the following two pages reveals a tremendous amount of information about HIV infection, both around the world and over time. Different colors show differing rates of infection around the world, smaller maps show the progress of infections since 1990, and the columns of numbers on the right provide data about how many people are infected and where HIV is most prevalent.

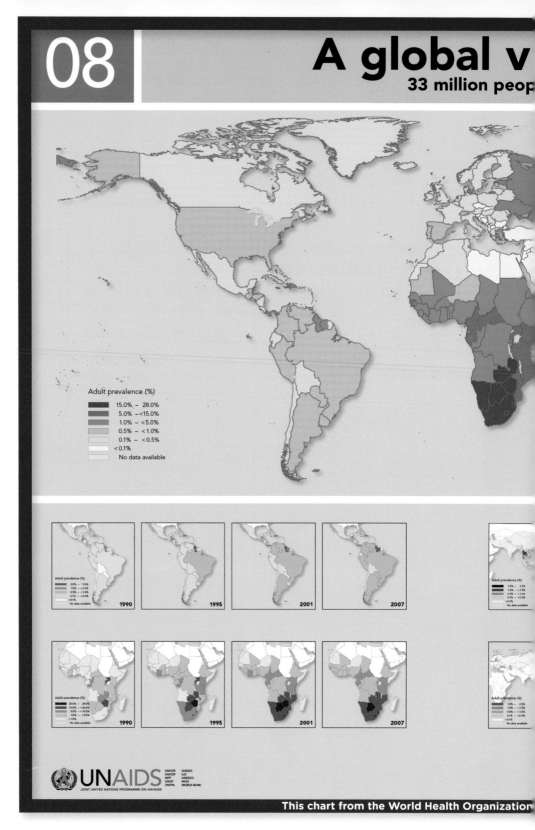

Adult prevalence (%)

15.0% – 28.0%
5.0% – <15.0%
1.0% – <5.0%
0.5% – <1.0%
0.1% – <0.5%
<0.1%
No data available

1990   1995   2001   2007

1990   1995   2001   2007

UNAIDS
JOINT UNITED NATIONS PROGRAMME ON HIV/AIDS

UNHCR   UNODC
UNICEF   ILO
WFP   UNESCO
UNDP   WHO
UNFPA   WORLD BANK

This chart from the World Health Organization

Estimated adult (15-49) HIV prevalence (%) for countries in...

Country/Region	Estimate	[low estimate – high estimate]	Country/Region	Estimate	[high...]
Sub-Saharan Africa			Lithuania	0.1	
Angola	2.1	[1.7 – 2.5]	Republic of Moldova	0.4	
Benin	1.2	[1.1 – 1.4]	Romania	0.1	
Botswana	23.9	[22.5 – 24.9]	Russian Federation	1.1	
Burkina Faso	1.6	[1.4 – 1.9]	Tajikistan	0.3	
Burundi	2.0	[1.3 – 2.5]	Turkmenistan	<0.1	
Cameroon	5.1	[3.9 – 6.2]	Ukraine	1.6	
Central African Republic	6.3	[5.9 – 6.7]	Uzbekistan	0.1	
Chad	3.5	[2.4 – 4.3]	**Western and Central Europe**		
Comoros	<0.1	[0.1]	Albania	...	
Congo	3.5	[2.8 – 4.2]	Austria	0.2	
Côte d'Ivoire	3.9	[3.2 – 4.5]	Belgium	0.2	
Democratic Republic of Congo	...	[1.2 – 1.5]	Czech Republic	...	
Djibouti	3.1	[2.3 – 3.8]	Denmark	0.2	
Equatorial Guinea	3.4	[2.6 – 4.6]	Finland	0.1	
Eritrea	1.3	[0.8 – 2.0]	France	0.4	
Ethiopia	2.1	[1.8 – 2.2]	Germany	0.1	
Gabon	5.9	[4.4 – 8.3]	Greece	0.2	
Gambia	0.9	[0.4 – 1.3]	Hungary	0.1	
Ghana	1.9	[1.7 – 2.2]	Iceland	0.3	
Guinea	1.6	[1.3 – 2.2]	Ireland	0.2	
Guinea–Bissau	1.8	[1.3 – 2.6]	Israel	0.1	
Kenya	...	[7.1 – 8.5]	Italy	0.4	
Lesotho	23.2	[21.9 – 24.5]	Luxembourg	0.2	
Liberia	1.7	[1.4 – 2.0]	Malta	0.1	
Madagascar	0.1	[<0.1 – 0.2]	Montenegro	...	
Malawi	11.9	[11.0 – 12.9]	Netherlands	0.2	
Mali	1.5	[1.2 – 1.8]	Norway	0.1	
Mauritania	0.8	[0.5 – 1.5]	Poland	0.1	
Mauritius	1.7	[1.0 – 3.6]	Portugal	0.5	
Mozambique	12.5	[10.9 – 14.7]	Serbia	0.1	
Namibia	15.3	[12.4 – 18.1]	Slovakia	<0.1	
Niger	0.8	[0.6 – 1.1]	Slovenia	<0.1	
Nigeria	3.1	[2.3 – 3.8]	Spain	0.5	
Rwanda	2.8	[2.4 – 3.2]	Sweden	0.1	
Senegal	1.0	[0.7 – 1.4]	Switzerland	0.6	
Sierra Leone	1.7	[1.3 – 2.4]	The former Yugoslav Republic of Macedonia	<0.1	
Somalia	0.5	[0.3 – 1.0]	United Kingdom of Great Britain and Northern Ireland	0.2	
South Africa	18.1	[15.4 – 20.9]	**North Africa and Middle East**		
Swaziland	26.1	[25.1 – 27.1]	Algeria	0.1	
Togo	3.3	[2.7 – 4.1]	Bahrain	...	
Uganda	5.4	[5.0 – 6.1]	Cyprus	...	
United Republic of Tanzania	6.2	[5.8 – 6.6]	Egypt	...	
Zambia	15.2	[14.3 – 16.4]	Iraq	...	
Zimbabwe	15.3	[14.6 – 16.1]	Jordan	...	
East Asia			Kuwait	...	
China	0.1	[<0.1 – 0.2]	Lebanon	0.1	
Democratic People's Republic of Korea	...	[<0.1]	Libyan Arab Jamahiriya	...	
Japan	...	[<0.1]	Morocco	0.1	
Mongolia	0.1	[<0.1 – 0.2]	Oman	...	
Republic of Korea	<0.1	[0.1]	Qatar	...	
Oceania			Saudi Arabia	...	
Australia	0.2	[0.1 – 0.3]	Sudan	1.4	
Fiji	0.1	[<0.1 – <0.2]	Syrian Arab Republic	...	
New Zealand	0.1	[<0.1 – 0.2]	Tunisia	0.1	
Papua New Guinea	1.5	[1.4 – 1.6]	Turkey	...	
South and South–East Asia			United Arab Emirates	...	
Afghanistan	...	[<0.2]	Yemen	...	
Bangladesh	...	[<0.1]	**North America**		
Bhutan	0.1	[<0.1 – 0.2]	Canada	0.4	
Brunei Darussalam	...		United States of America	0.6	
Cambodia	0.8	[0.7 – 0.9]	**Caribbean**		
India	0.3	[0.2 – 0.5]	Bahamas	3.0	
Indonesia	0.2	[0.1 – 0.3]	Barbados	1.2	
Iran (Islamic Republic of)	0.2	[0.1 – 0.3]	Cuba	0.1	
Lao People's Democratic Republic	0.2	[0.1 – 0.4]	Dominican Republic	1.1	
Malaysia	0.5	[0.3 – 0.8]	Haiti	2.2	
Maldives	...	[<0.1]	Jamaica	1.6	
Myanmar	0.7	[0.4 – 1.1]	Trinidad and Tobago	1.5	
Nepal	0.5	[0.4 – 0.7]	**Latin America**		
Pakistan	0.1	[<0.1 – 0.2]	Argentina	0.5	
Philippines	...	[<0.1]	Belize	2.1	
Singapore	0.2	[0.1 – 0.3]	Bolivia	0.2	
Sri Lanka	...	[<0.1]	Brazil	0.6	
Thailand	1.4	[0.9 – 2.1]	Chile	0.3	
Timor–Leste	...		Colombia	0.6	
Viet Nam	0.5	[0.3 – 0.9]	Costa Rica	0.4	
Eastern Europe and Central Asia			Ecuador	0.3	
Armenia	0.1	[<0.1 – 0.2]	El Salvador	0.8	
Azerbaijan	0.2	[<0.1 – 0.3]	Guatemala	0.8	
Belarus	0.2	[0.1 – 0.3]	Guyana	2.5	
Bosnia and Herzegovina	<0.1	[<0.2]	Honduras	0.7	
Bulgaria	...	[<0.2]	Mexico	0.3	
Croatia	<0.1	[<0.2]	Nicaragua	0.2	
Estonia	1.3	[0.7 – 2.5]	Panama	1.0	
Georgia	0.1	[<0.1 – 0.3]	Paraguay	0.6	
Kazakhstan	0.1	[<0.1 – 0.3]	Peru	0.5	
Kyrgyzstan	0.1	[<0.1 – 0.3]	Suriname	2.4	
Latvia	0.8	[0.6 – 1.2]	Uruguay	0.6	
			Venezuela	...	

To calculate the adult HIV prevalence rate, the estimated number of adults (15–49) living with HIV in 2007 was... 2007 population (aged 15–49).

Depending on the reliability of the data available, there is more or less certainty surrounding any one estim... we present ranges, called 'plausibility bounds' around the estimates. The wider the bound, the more un... is surrounding the country's estimate. The extent of uncertainty depends mainly on the type of epidemic, a... coverage and consistency of a country's surveillance system and in generalized epidemics, whether or not a po... survey with HIV testing was conducted. A full description of the methods used to develop plausibility bounds c... *Sexually Transmitted Infections*, 2008, 84 (Supp I).

These estimates are the product of UNAIDS/WHO. The estimates have been shared with national AIDS program... and comments, but are not necessarily the official estimates used by national governments.

The designations employed and the presentation of the material in this map, including tables and colouring of... do not imply the expression of any opinion whatsoever on the part of UNAIDS or WHO concerning the leg... country, territory, city or area or of its authorities, or concerning the delimitation of its frontiers or boundaries.

Source: 2008 Report on the global AIDS epidemic. ...

World Health Organization

view of the 33 million people living with HIV.

CHAPTER SEVEN

Living With STDs

No one chooses to have an STD. But before most people become infected with an STD they usually make a choice, although a poor one. Maybe, in the heat of the moment, they decide to have unprotected sex with someone they barely know. Or maybe they decide to trust someone they think they know well when he or she says, "I don't have any diseases," so they do not use a condom.

Living with an STD also involves choices. People can decide to let the infection take over their lives. Or they can decide to live their best lives in spite of having an STD.

"There were so many times I thought life just wasn't worth living because I was some kind of leper," says Carly, who has been living with herpes for fifteen years and is a moderator for an online herpes support group. "It took some time, but I finally realized that herpes didn't define me. It was simply a skin condition that I had to live with."[1]

THE FIRST STEPS

Sexually transmitted diseases range from embarrassing annoyances (like pubic lice) to lifelong but not life-threatening infections (like herpes), to deadly diseases (like AIDS). But all STDs have this in common: They require diagnosis and treatment. For many people, the first steps are the hardest to take.

Someone who is living with an STD can decide to let the infection take over her life, or she can choose to live her best life despite being infected with an STD.

Be honest with your partner about an STD; he or she may care enough to continue the relationship.

FINDING THE COURAGE TO TELL SEX PARTNERS

Notifying a current or past sex partner or partners can be scary, and some can find it humiliating. Making the phone call or having the face-to-face talk is easier if newly diagnosed people give themselves a few days to calm down, read the information the doctor gave them, and start coming to terms with the fact that they have an STD.

Carly says: "Most of the time 'The Talk' turns out well. You'll even get 'So what? So do I!' after delivering the news."[2]

For more tips on breaking the news to partners, see Chapter 5.

STARTING TO MOVE ON

When people hear they have an STD, their self-image takes a nosedive. They feel ashamed, embarrassed, scared, and alone. They may feel dirty and unhealthy and think that no one will ever want to have sex with them again. These are all normal reactions. But eventually, most people put things into perspective and realize their lives are not over. How do they do this?

- **By becoming "experts."** After people are diagnosed, they usually read everything they can find about their STD. Besides studying the written materials provided by their doctor, they also visit dozens of Internet sites and read up on the causes, diagnoses, prevention, and treatment of STDs.

- **By communicating online.** Many STD sites have message boards where people can share stories and "talk" with other people who have the same STD. Message boards provide a sense of community and help people feel that they are not alone.

- **By communicating in person.** Talking to someone in person is a good idea, too. People may confide in one close friend or family member they know they can trust, or they may decide to talk to a professional counselor. Planned Parenthood and clinics that specialize in STDs provide counseling services. Many hospitals and clinics also offer support groups for people with STDs. These informal meetings provide a way for people to meet, share their stories, and receive advice and news about the latest treatments.

MEETING THE STD CHALLENGE

People living with chronic STDs face many more challenges than those whose infections can be wiped out with medication. But all people diagnosed with STDs go through emotional turmoil and have important decisions to make. Depending on the STD, they have to face questions about sexual relationships, pregnancy and childbirth, long-term complications, and more. Their lives may be changed by their STD, but they are not over.

HOW REAL PEOPLE DEAL: RYAN WHITE'S BATTLE

Every teenager dreams of being famous, but Ryan White's fame came at a price. When he was thirteen, the Indiana teenager contracted the AIDS virus through contaminated medicine and was told he only had six months to live. He beat the odds and lived six more years, but he fought one battle after another just trying to be a normal kid.

Ryan had always been a fighter. Diagnosed with severe hemophilia as an infant, he managed to live a relatively normal childhood with the help of injections and transfusions of a drug called Factorate that helped his blood clot. In 1984, Ryan found out the lifesaving drug, which contained blood, had given him HIV.

He spent the next month lying in a hospital bed, planning how to spend what little time he had left. He decided to lead a normal life, go to school, and spend time with friends. But little was known about AIDS in those days, and fear and ignorance caused the community to turn against Ryan and his family. He was not allowed to attend school, although he finally won the right after a highly publicized nine-month court battle. But after he returned to school, he had to use a separate restroom and drinking fountain, eat with disposable utensils, and not attend gym class. Restaurants threw away his dishes, and even in church, people shunned him.

But while Ryan was shunned at home, the news media embraced him. He appeared on *Good Morning America* and other TV shows and was on the cover of *People* magazine three times. A movie was made about his life. He met celebrities such as Elton John and Charlie Sheen. He made public appearances, including testifying before the National Commission on AIDS. He spoke on behalf of all people with HIV and AIDS who only wanted to be treated like everyone else. Even though he

Continued on next page

Continued from previous page

contracted the virus through a blood product and not sexually or by sharing needles, he refused to be portrayed as an innocent victim and never set himself apart from people who had contracted AIDS in other ways.

In 1987, Ryan and his family moved to Cicero, Indiana, to make a new life for themselves. The community welcomed them with open arms. Ryan attended high school, made new friends, made the honor roll, learned to drive, and was a normal teenager again.

"Hamilton Heights High School is proof that AIDS education in schools works," Ryan said in a speech to the National Education Association in 1988. "Teachers can play an important role in helping AIDS students be accepted and treated as normal as possible by teaching the facts, not the myths. By proper education, AIDS can be a disease, not a dirty word."[3]

Ryan died in 1990, a few months before he would have graduated from high school. His funeral was attended by First Lady Barbara Bush and was the one of the largest in the state's history. Ryan's memory lives on in programs like the Ryan White CARE Act, which funds services for half a million people with HIV/AIDS each year.

Today, under the Americans with Disabilities Act, people with HIV or AIDS cannot be barred from schools or workplaces. Now we understand much more about HIV and AIDS, thanks to pioneers like Ryan White, a young man who dedicated his short life to helping others.[4]

Laura Bush stands by President George W. Bush as he signs the Ryan White HIV/AIDS Treatment Modernization Act of 2006 (the Ryan White CARE Act), which funds services for half a million people with HIV/AIDS.

WORK AND SCHOOL

A person with an STD is not obligated to share this information with employers, teachers, or anyone except sex partners they might have infected. Those with HIV are covered under the Americans with Disabilities Act, a federal law that states employers cannot fire or refuse to hire a qualified person because he has a disability.[5] Students with HIV cannot be discriminated against in schools, either, and no cases of HIV have ever been transmitted in the school setting.[6]

A person with an STD is not obligated to share this information with employers, teachers, or anyone except sex partners they might have infected.

However, some people may choose to tell their employers if they have HIV and get a letter from their doctor saying they need to take certain medicines while at work, take rest breaks, or leave work for medical appointments. Parents of children with HIV should talk to the school principal, school nurse, and the child's teachers to discuss the child's special needs. In both cases, the person with the STD has the right to confidentiality, meaning the employer or school officials cannot share the person's health information with anyone else.[7]

SEX AND DATING

People with curable STDs like chlamydia, who have been treated and are free of disease, do not have to tell future sex partners they were once infected. It is their choice. But people with chronic STDs like herpes or HPV must tell all future partners before starting a sexual relationship. It is called having "The Talk" in STD circles, and it is never easy. But people with STDs are having the talk and meeting this challenge every day.

If a person plans to practice safer sex, why does he need to have The Talk with future sex partners? Here is why: Sex is *never* hundred percent safe; it is possible to transmit STDs even when using protection. Potential partners deserve to know all the facts before entering into a sexual relationship. They will be glad they were told the truth and respect the other person for caring enough about them to be honest. If they find out about the STD later, or worse yet, catch it, they will feel betrayed and will probably end the relationship.

Of course, those with STDs need to prepare themselves for the possibility of being rejected. But then, so do people who do not have STDs. More often than not, people with STDs discover that the other person cares enough to continue the relationship; maybe the honest discussion even brings the couple closer together. As Carly observed, sometimes the other person even admits he or she has the same STD!

When should people divulge their STD status? Definitely not on the first date. Couples need to get to know one another first and then decide whether pursuing a sexual relationship is what they both want. Waiting too long is a mistake, too. Saying, "I have herpes" on the way to the bedroom is a big turnoff, to say the least. The other person needs time to let the information sink in before making such an important decision.

How should a person approach the topic of having an STD? Calmly and armed with information. They should hand the other person brochures about the infection and safer sex practices and answer any questions. They might also tell the other person where to go for counseling if they want to learn more about the infection and offer to go with them.

It goes without saying that practicing safer sex is more important than ever when one person is infected with an STD. People should not have sex at all when they have genital warts or during an outbreak of herpes blisters. They should not have sex at all until their blood tests negative for acute hepatitis B. This is not just to protect their partners, but also to protect themselves. People who already have an STD are more vulnerable to catching another one. People with HIV are especially susceptible because their immune systems are weakened from the virus.

For more information on practicing safer sex, see Chapter 4.

When should people divulge their STD status? Definitely not on the first date. Couples need to get to know one another first and then decide whether pursuing a sexual relationship is what they both want.

PREGNANCY AND CHILDBIRTH

Many women with STDs, including herpes, HPV, and even HIV, can get pregnant and have healthy babies. But they will need to see their doctor often and take many precautions to prevent miscarriage, early labor, and other problems. A woman with HPV may need to have a cesarean delivery (c-section) if she has warts in her birth canal; otherwise, the baby could be infected during birth. The same is true for women with genital herpes. Women with HIV can reduce the chance of transmitting the AIDS virus to their unborn babies by taking drugs such as AZT during pregnancy, having c-sections, and not breastfeeding. Other women with STDs may also be prescribed drugs during pregnancy, such as acyclovir for a severe outbreak of herpes.

A woman with HPV may need to have a cesarean delivery (c-section) if she has warts in her birth canal; otherwise, the baby could be infected during birth.

Some STDs can also cause infertility in men and women. Young, sexually active women are probably trying *not* to get pregnant, but contracting an STD may prevent them from getting pregnant later, when they feel the time is right. For example, one episode of PID caused by chlamydia cuts a woman's chances of becoming pregnant by twenty percent. Regular STD testing spots infections early, before they damage the reproductive organs.[8]

For more information on pregnancy and childbirth, see Chapter 2.

HEALTH INSURANCE AND MEDICAL COSTS

Health insurance companies may label people as "high risk" if they have been tested for AIDS, hepatitis B, or certain other STDs, even if the results were negative. They can cancel existing health insurance policies or refuse to give new insurance policies to people. This keeps a lot of people from being tested. One way to get around this is to go to a clinic that does anonymous testing and then pay in cash and tell the clinic not to bill the insurance company.

Blood Transfusions Cause AIDS

Not anymore. Tragically, some people did contract HIV from blood transfusions in the early 1980s. But today, the U.S. blood supply is among the safest in the world. Since 1985, when donated blood started being tested for HIV, the risk has dropped to between one in 450,000 and one in 660,000.[9]

Donated blood is also screened for hepatitis B and C and syphilis. Blood that tests positive for these infections or HIV is safely disposed of. Then the Red Cross or other blood collection agency writes a letter to the donor, informing him that he may have the infection. Besides people with HIV, people who had hepatitis B or C can never donate blood. The Red Cross recommends that people wait twelve months to donate blood after being treated for syphilis or gonorrhea.

Donated blood is screened for HIV as well as other STDs before it is used for a transfusion.

Drugs used to treat HIV and AIDS are also very expensive, but several drug companies have programs that provide lower-cost drugs to people who cannot afford to pay for HIV and AIDS drug regimens, which can cost hundreds or thousands of dollars a month.

PHYSICAL AND MENTAL HEALTH

Besides the difficulties with pregnancy and childbirth discussed above, chronic STDs can present other physical challenges as well as taking an emotional toll. Only a small percentage of women with HPV get cervical cancer, but the possibility always looms. Compared to cancer, herpes outbreaks are not serious, but worrying about when the next outbreak will occur can be

Highly social teens who date a lot need to be aware of STDs. Information about transmission, diagnosis, and treatment is important for everyone who is or may become sexually active.

nerve-wracking. People with HIV or AIDS may feel like they live from one blood test to the next, wondering if their cell counts are too low, wondering if the next infection or illness is the one they will not survive.

Besides the drugs and other treatments discussed in Chapter 5, people with HIV/AIDS and other chronic STDs can bolster their immune systems by not smoking, not taking illegal drugs, eating nutritious foods, exercising, limiting alcohol, getting plenty of sleep, reducing stress, and seeing their doctors regularly. People with hepatitis B may also need several weeks of rest and should not drink alcohol or take any drugs that can damage the liver, often for the rest of their lives. They should also get a hepatitis A shot.

People with herpes and HPV should especially avoid stress, because it is thought to trigger outbreaks of blisters or warts. Smoking has also been linked to genital wart outbreaks—another reason not to light up! Diets low in folate may also cause warts, so people are encouraged to eat lots of green, leafy vegetables and take a multivitamin containing folic acid every day. Women with HPV should go for regular PAP tests to check for cell changes that signal cervical cancer.

CHALLENGES FOR FAMILIES

Sexually transmitted diseases never affect just one person, they always affect many people—and not just sex partners. The lives of people who live in the same household are also changed when someone they love has an STD. The change can range from a minor annoyance (having to wash clothes and bedding because of pubic lice) to a major upheaval (having to support a mom, wife, or sister through cervical cancer diagnosis and surgery). But no matter how minor and curable or major and chronic an STD is, when family members learn about the infection, their lives change.

TREPIDATION FOR TEENS

The diagnosis of an STD may be the first evidence that a teenager is having sex. Many parents avoid talking to their children about sex, so they are totally unprepared when a son or daughter gets an STD. That is, if the young person even tells them. Many teens are afraid to let their parents know, so they get tested on their own. Although clinics like Planned Parenthood keep information confidential, teens often decide to tell parents after a positive diagnosis is made. In most instances, parents offer emotional support (as well as financial) and help a teen get through this difficult time. When one teen girl found out she had HPV, her mom was supportive and helped her deal with the issue after her diagnosis.

"When I finally broke down and told my mom, she was there for me and let me cry on her shoulder," says the teen. "She asked me why I thought she'd be disappointed in me."[10]

CONCERNS FOR COUPLES

If one person in a couple is diagnosed with an STD, this can put a tremendous strain on the relationship. After the shock of the diagnosis, the first question people ask themselves is, "Did my (husband, wife, partner) cheat?" Blaming the other person is common, and sometimes, the other person *is* to blame. On the other hand, many STDs have no symptoms or can lie dormant for years, so a partner can pass them on without being unfaithful. Either way, the diagnosis of an STD can test a relationship. If there are children or other people in the household, they suffer, too. Some couples find that therapy helps them get past the diagnosis and keep their relationship together.

FACTS FOR HOUSEHOLD MEMBERS

Most STDs cannot be passed on by casual contact, but family members need to take precautions with HIV and hepatitis B, which are transmitted by blood. If a person in the household has hepatitis B, people should not share toothbrushes, razors, nail clippers, or anything that might have blood on it. The hepatitis B virus survives for quite a while outside the body, and blood exposure can occur unknowingly, so all close family members should get a hepatitis B shot within fourteen days of exposure. Infected people should cover any open sores and rashes.

The AIDS virus does not survive long outside the body, but blood exposure should still be avoided, using the above precautions. Neither of these infections can be transmitted by sharing dishes or toilet seats, unless they are contaminated with blood. Any blood spills should be cleaned up immediately with a solution of one part bleach to ten parts water.

People living in the same house cannot catch herpes, HPV, and other STDs through nonsexual means. However, people with cold sores (HSV-1) on their lips should not kiss other people, even on the cheek. Some experts think trichomoniasis can be transmitted by sharing towels or bathing suits, so avoiding this might be a good idea. Households can also be infested with scabies and pubic lice, which are passed from one person to another via clothes and bedding.

SURVIVING SOCIAL STIGMA

It is possible to be diagnosed, treated, and cured of an STD without anyone knowing except the person's doctor and sexual partner or partners. People can put these kinds of STDs behind them and practice safer sex forever after. Unfortunately, some STDs are more obvious, particularly HIV or AIDS. People with this infection are often so ill that they cannot keep their disease a secret.

Although laws now protect them from being discriminated against at work or at school, people with the HIV virus continue to be regarded with fear, even though the virus is not contagious through casual contact. Because HIV almost always infected gay men in the early years, prejudice against homosexuality added to the social stigma. That is no longer the case. Gay men make

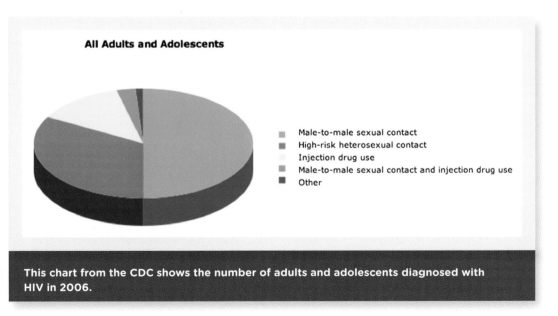

All Adults and Adolescents

■ Male-to-male sexual contact
■ High-risk heterosexual contact
  Injection drug use
■ Male-to-male sexual contact and injection drug use
■ Other

This chart from the CDC shows the number of adults and adolescents diagnosed with HIV in 2006.

up just slightly more than half of all HIV/AIDS cases in the United States, with heterosexual men and women and injection drug users constituting just under half.[11]

For most people with STDs, whose infections are not visible or life threatening, the feelings of shame are self-inflicted. The glamorized, sanitized picture of sex promoted in the movies and on TV leaves no room for discussions of STDs. This makes people who are infected feel tainted and alone, even though they have plenty of company. About 65 million Americans are living with STDs today![12]

People of all ages must learn the facts about STDs, get tested and treated if they catch one, and notify partners. Most important, they must practice safer sex. These are the only sure ways to wipe out this *preventable* epidemic.

STDs Timeline

c. 2200 B.C.: Sumerian tablet describes lesions and sores similar to those found in herpes.

c. 1550 B.C.: Ebers Papyrus, an Egyptian document, describes painful urination, a symptom of gonorrhea.

c. 300 B.C.: Greek physician Hippocrates refers to skin lesions as "herpes," which means "creep" or "crawl."

c. A.D. 100: Galen, a Greek physician, coins the term "gonorrhea," meaning "flow of seed."

1495: A syphilis epidemic begins that rages through Europe for the next few decades.

1527: French physician Jacques de Bethencourt calls syphilis "morbus venereus" (the sickness of Venus), from which the term *venereal disease* comes.

1530: Syphilis gets its name from a poem about a shepherd named Syphilis who gets the disease as a penalty for offending the gods.

1687: Giovan Bonomo, an Italian physician, draws a picture of the mite that causes scabies.

1736: John Astruc, physician for King Louis XIV of France, links herpes to the genital organs while studying French prostitutes.

1836: Alfred Donné discovers the protozoan parasite that causes trichomoniasis and names it *Trichomonas vaginalis*.

1837: French venereologist Philippe Ricord establishes that syphilis and gonorrhea are two different diseases. He later describes the three stages of syphilis.

1872: Emil Noeggerath, an American physician, discovers that gonorrhea can be latent in men but still communicable.

1873: Emile Vidal proves that herpes simplex virus (HSV) is an infectious disease.

1879: German dermatologist Albert Neisser discovers the bacterium that causes gonorrhea and calls it "gonococcus."

1881: German obstetrician Karl Credé discovers that some blindness in newborns is caused at birth, when the vaginal discharge of women with gonorrhea is directly transferred to the infant's eyes.

1883: Alfred Fournier, a French dermatologist, describes "congenital syphilis," a condition in which children inherit the disease but have no symptoms until later in life.

1905: German researchers Fritz Schaudinn and Erich Hoffmann discover the cause of syphilis, a spiral-shaped microorganism they call *Treponema pallidum*.

1906: August von Wassermann, a German bacteriologist, introduces a diagnostic test for syphilis.

1907: German researcher Ludwig Halberstaedter and Czech zoologist Stanislaus von Prowazek discover the bacterium for chlamydia by infecting orangutans with scrapings from the eyes of people with trachoma. They name it *Chlamydia trachomatis*.

1909: German researcher Paul Ehrlich discovers a "magic bullet" he calls Salvarsan, a synthetic arsenic compound that treats syphilis.

1928: Scottish scientist Alexander Fleming discovers penicillin, the first antibiotic.

1940: Australia-born Howard Florey and German-born Ernst Chain, researchers working together in Great Britain, discover how to purify penicillin so it can be manufactured.

1947: British physician F.O. MacCallum discovers that hepatitis B (HBV) is transferred by exposure to blood.

1962: Herpes virus is classified into two types, HSV-1 and HSV-2.

1970s: German virologist Harald zur Hausen discovers HPV 16 and HPV 18, two viruses that cause cervical cancer.

1981: Patients in the United States begin to become sick with the disease that comes to be known as AIDS.

1982: FDA approves first vaccine for hepatitis B.

1983: Doctors at the Pasteur Institute in France identify the retrovirus that causes AIDS.

1985: A blood test is discovered to diagnose the AIDS retrovirus.

1985: FDA approves acyclovir, the first genital herpes drug.

1986: The AIDS retrovirus is named human immunodeficiency virus (HIV).

1987: The FDA approves a drug named AZT to fight HIV/AIDS.

1995: FDA approves first vaccine for hepatitis A.

2006: FDA approves the first one-a-day pill to treat HIV/AIDS. A vaccine for HPV is approved.

Chapter Notes

Introduction

1. Centers for Disease Control and Prevention, "Health Topics: Sexual Risk Behaviors," <http://www.cdc.gov/healthyyouth/sexualbehaviors> (April 15, 2008).

Chapter 1: Straight Talk About STDs

1. Online interview with "Heather" (pseudonym), April 29, 2008.

2. Centers for Disease Control and Prevention, "Health Topics: Sexual Risk Behaviors," <http://www.cdc.gov/healthyyouth/sexualbehaviors> (April 15, 2008).

3. The Free Library, "Coffee, tea, or bacteria?" (Health/Bacteria), <http://www.thefreelibrary.com/Coffee, tea, or bacteria? (Health/Bacteria)-a097235870> (April 23, 2008).

4. Healthline, "Sexually Transmitted Diseases," <http://www.healthline.com/gale-content/sexually-transmitted-diseases> (March 17, 2008).

5. WrongDiagnosis, "Statistics about Common Cold," <http://www.wrongdiagnosis.com/c/cold/stats/htm> (May 25, 2008).

6. American Social Health Association, "STD/STI Statistics: Fast Facts," <http://www.ashastd.org/learn/learn_statistics.cfm> (March 16, 2008).

7. Centers for Disease Control and Prevention, "Opportunity to Educate Teens Often Overlooked, According to CDC Study," <http://www.cdc.gov/nchstp/dstd/Press_Releases/Teens2000.html> (April 23, 2008).

8. Avert.org, "STD Statistics Worldwide," <http://www.avert.org/stdstatisticsworldwide.htm> (April 22, 2008).

9. Centers for Disease Control and Prevention, "Revised Final FY 1999 Performance Plan and FY 2000 Performance Plan, IV. Infectious Diseases, Sexually Transmitted Diseases," <http://www.cdc.gov/od/perfplan/2000/2000ivSTD.htm> (April 22, 2008).

10. MedlinePlus, "Bacterial Infections," <http://www.nlm.nih.gov/medlineplus/bacterialinfections.html> (April 15, 2008).

Chapter 2: The Science of STDs

1. National Prevention Information Network, "STDs Today," <http://www.cdcpin.org/scripts/std/std.asp> (March 16, 2008).

2. Centers for Disease Control and Prevention, "Trends in Reportable Sexually Transmitted Diseases in the United States, 2006: National Surveillance Data for Chlamydia, Gonorrhea, and Syphilis," <http://www.cdc.gov/std/stats/trends2006.htm> (May 5, 2008).

3. Planned Parenthood, "Chlamydia," <http://www.plannedparenthood.org/health-topics/stds-hiv-safer-sex/chlamydia-4266.htm> (April 27, 2008).

4. A Case of Chlamydia, adapted from "I Had a Sexually Transmitted Disease," by Tori Smart, as told to Sandi Fertman, *Teen*, November, 1997, pp. 63–64.

5. Centers for Disease Control and Prevention, "Trends in Reportable Sexually Transmitted Diseases in the United States, 2006: National Surveillance Data for Chlamydia, Gonorrhea, and Syphilis," <http://www.cdc.gov/std/stats/trends2006.htm> pp. 3–4 (May 5, 2008).

6. Lisa Marr, M.D., *Sexually Transmitted Diseases: A Physician Tells You What You Need to Know*, Second Edition (Baltimore: The Johns Hopkins University Press, 2007), p. 178.

7. Marr, p. 287.

8. Centers for Disease Control and Prevention, "Pelvic Inflammatory Disease – CDC Fact Sheet," <http://www.cdc.gov/STD/PID/STDFact-PID.htm> (May 7, 2008).

9. Intelihealth, "Epididymitis and Orchitis," <http://www.intelihealth.com/IHihtIH/WS/9339/10467.html> (May 10, 2008).

10. National Prevention Information Network, "STDs Today," <http://www.cdcnpin.org/scripts/std/std.asp> (March 16, 2008).

11. Planned Parenthood, "Hepatitis B," <http://www.plannedparenthood.org/health-topics/stds-hiv-safer-sex/hepatitis-b-4270.htm> (May 6, 2008).

12. Centers for Disease Control and Prevention, "Genital Herpes – CDC Fact Sheet," <http://www.cdc.gov/STD/Herpes?STDFact-Herpes.htm> (May 6, 2008).

13. Centers for Disease Control and Prevention, "HIV/AIDS in the United States," <http://www.cdc.gov/hiv/resources/factsheets/us.htm> (May 7, 2008).

14. Planned Parenthood, "HIV/AIDS," <http://www.plannedparenthood.org/health-topics/stds-hiv-safer-sex/hiv-aids-4264.htm> (May 7, 2008).

15. Centers for Disease Control and Prevention, "Genital HPV Infection – CDC Fact Sheet," <http://www.cdc.gov/STD/HPV/STDFact-JPV.htm> (May 7, 2008).

16. Centers for Disease Control and Prevention, "Genital HPV Infection – CDC Fact Sheet," <http://www.cdc.gov/std/HPV/STDFact-HPV.htm> (December 19, 2008).

17. Planned Parenthood, "HPV," <http://www.plannedparenthood.org/health-topics/stds-hiv-safer-sex/hpv-4272.htm> (May 7, 2008).

18. Marr, p. 297.

19. Centers for Disease Control and Prevention, "Syphilis – CDC Fact Sheet," <http://www.cdc.gov/STD/Syphilis/STDFact-Syphilis.htm> (May 7, 2008).

20. Centers for Disease Control and Prevention, "Syphilis – CDC Fact Sheet," <http://www.cdc.gov/STD/syphilis/STDFact-syphilis.htm> (May 7, 2008).

21. Centers for Disease Control and Prevention, "Trichomoniasis – CDC Fact Sheet," <http://www.cdc.gov/STD/Syphilis/STDFact-Syphilis.htm> (May 7, 2008).

22. National Women's Health Information Center, "Trichomoniasis," <http://www.womenshealth.gov/faq/stdtrich.htm> (May 18, 2008).

Chapter 3: The History of STDs

1. Mark Rose, "Origins of Syphilis," *Archaeology*, Vol. 50, No. 1, January/February 1997, <http://www.archaeology.org/9701/newsbriefs/syphilis.html> (May 1, 2008).

2. Lois N. Magner, et al, "Historic Dispute: Did syphilis originate in the New World, from which it was brought to Europe by Christopher Columbus and his crew?" *Science Clarified: Science in Dispute:* Vol. 2 (2002), <http://www.scienceclarified.com/dispute/Vol-2/Historic-Dispute-Did-syphilis-originate-in-the-New-World-from-which-it-was-brought-to-Europe-by-Christopher-Columbus-and-his-crew.html> (May 1, 2008).

3. Alfred W. Crosby, Jr., "The Early History of Syphilis: A Reappraisal," *American Anthropologist*, April 1969, Vol. 71, No. 2, pp. 218–227, <http://www.anthrosource.net/doi/abs/10.1525/aa.1969.71.2.02a00020> (May 29, 2008).

4. Allan M. Brandt, *No Magic Bullet: A Social History of Venereal Disease in the United States Since 1880* (New York: Oxford University Press, 1987), p. 11.

5. Peter M. Dunn, "Dr. Carl Credé (1819–1892) and the prevention of ophthalmia neonatorum," *Archives of Disease in Childhood: Fetal and Neonatal Ed.,* September 2000, Vol. 83, pp. 158–159, <http://www.pubmedcentral.nih.gov/picrender.fcgi?artid=1721147&blobtype=pdf> (May 1, 2008).

6. Laura Parker, "'Bad Blood' Still Flows in Tuskegee Study," *USA Today*, April 28, 1997, <http://www.libarts.ucok.edu/history/faculty/roberson/course/1493/readings/Tuskegee%20Experiment.htm> (May 27, 2008).

7. Brandt, p. 115.

8. "Visual Culture and Public Health Posters: Infectious Disease: Venereal Disease," *National Library of Medicine*, 2003, p. 2, <http://www.nlm.nih.gov/exhibition/visualculture/venereal.html> (May 6, 2008).

9. AIDS Education Global Information System, "So little time…An AIDS History," <http://www.aegis.com/topics/timeline/> (May 9, 2008).

10. AIDS Origins, "Edward Hooper – A Brief Bio," <http://www.aidsorigins.com/content/view/23/30> (May 26, 2008).

11. Scott Norris, "Gorillas Gave Pubic Lice to Humans, DNA Study Reveals," *National Geographic News*, March 16, 2007, <http://www.news.nationalgeographic.com/news/2007/03/070316-gorilla-lice.html> (May 1, 2008).

12. Marcia Ramos-e-Silva, MD, PhD, "Giovan Cosimo Bonomo (1663–1696): Discoverer of the etiology of scabies," *International Journal of Dermatology*, 1998, 7(8): pp. 625–630, <http://www.dermato.med.br/hds/bibliography/1998giovan-cosimo-bonomo.htm> (May 7, 2008).

Chapter 4: Preventing STDs

1. Avert.Org, "STD Statistics for the USA," <http://www.avert.org/stdstatisticusa.htm> (May 15, 2008).

2. Centers for Disease Control and Prevention, "Trends in Reportable Sexually Transmitted Diseases in the United States, 2006," November 14, 2007. <http://www.cdc.gov/std/stats/trends2006.htm> (May 15, 2008).

3. National Prevention Information Network, "STDs Today," <http://www.cdcnpin.org/scripts/std/std.asp> (May 15, 2008).

4. Centers for Disease Control and Prevention. "Sexually Transmitted Diseases (STDs)," 2005, <http://www.cdc.gov/nchhstp/healthdisparities/STDs.htm> (May 19, 2008).

5. Centers for Disease Control and Prevention, "Healthy Youth: Sexual Risk Behaviors," <http://www.cdc.gov/HealthyYouth/sexualbehaviors/> (May 15, 2008).

6. Terry Wynn, "Social Issues Linked to Rise in STDs," *MSNBC*, April 20, 2005, <http://www.msnbc.msn.com/id/7268133/> (May 15, 2008).

7. "Prevalence of Sexually Transmitted Infections and Bacterial Vaginosis among Female Adolescents in the United States: Data from the National Health and Nutritional Examination Survey (NHANES) 2003–2004," *2008 National STD Prevention Conference*, March 11, 2008, <http://www.cdc.gov/stdconference/2008/media/summaries-11march2008.htm#tues1> (May 16, 2008).

8. Centers for Disease Control and Prevention, "Healthy Youth: Sexual Risk Behaviors," <http://www.cdc.gov/HealthyYouth/sexualbehaviors/> (May 15, 2008).

9. Ceci Connolly, "Teen Pledges Barely Cut STD Rates, Study Says," *The Washington Post*, March 19, 2005, p. A03, <http://www.washingtonpost.com/wp-dyn/articles/A48509-2005Mar18.html> (May 15, 2008).

10. U.S. Department of Health and Human Services, "National Institute of Allergy and Infectious Diseases, Workshop Summary: Scientific Evidence on Condom Effectiveness for Sexually Transmitted Disease (STD) Prevention," 2001, <http://www.niaid.nih.gov/research/topics/STI/pdf/condomreport.pdf> (May 16, 2008).

11. Centers for Disease Control and Prevention, "Fact Sheet for Public Health Personnel: Male Latex Condoms and Sexually Transmitted Diseases," January 23, 2003, <http://www.cdc.gov/condomeffectiveness/latex.htm> (May 16, 2008).

12. Lisa Marr, M.D., *Sexually Transmitted Diseases: A Physician Tells You What You Need To Know,* Second Edition (Baltimore: The Johns Hopkins University Press, 2007), pp. 102–103.

13. "Condoms and Safe Sex," *Postgraduate Medicine*, Vol. 107, No. 4, April 2000, <http://www.postgradmed.com/issues/2000/04_00/pn_condoms.shtml> (May 18, 2008).

14. National Social Health Association, "STD/STI Statistics: Fast Facts," <http://www.ashastd.org/learn/learn_statistics.cfm> (May 16, 2008).

15. S. E. Karpiak, et al, *Research on Older Adults with HIV*. New York: AIDS Community Research Initiative of America, 2006, p. 12, <http://www.acria.org/clinical/roah_05_05_08_final.pdf> (May 19, 2008).

16. Ibid.

17. Brigham Young University, "Sex, Drugs And Alcohol: Parents Still Influence College Kids' Risky Behavior, Study Shows," *ScienceDaily*, February 11, 2008, <http://www.sciencedaily.com/releases/2008/02/080210094643.htm> (May 16, 2008).

18. J. R. Cates, et al, *Our Voices, Our Lives, Our Futures: Youth and Sexually Transmitted Diseases*, (2004) Chapel Hill, NC: School of Journalism and Mass Communication, University of North Carolina at Chapel Hill, pp. 14–21, <http://www.ihc.unc.edu/ourvoicesreport.pdf> (May 16, 2008).

19. Centers for Disease Control and Prevention, "Chlamydia Screening Among Sexually Active Young Female Enrollees of Health Plans—United States, 1999–2001" *MMWR Weekly*, October 29, 2004, Vol. 53, No. 42, pp. 983–985. <http://www.cdc.gov/mmwr/preview/mmwrhtml/mm5342a1.htm> (August 18, 2009).

20. Ibid.

21. Centers for Disease Control and Prevention, "HPV Vaccine Questions and Answers," August 2006, <http://www.cdc.gov/std/hpv/STDFact-HPV-vaccine-young-women.htm> (June 26, 2008).

Chapter 5: Testing and Treatment

1. Carolyn's Place, "How Safe is Safe Sex—Really?" <http://www.carolynsplace.net/STD.ht> (April 27, 2008).

2. Centers for Disease Control and Prevention, National HIV and STD Testing Resources, "Frequently Asked Questions: Who Should Be Tested for STDs?" <http://www.hivtest.org/popups/faq.cfm#stdtest> (May 13, 2008).

3. Planned Parenthood, "Planned Parenthood at a Glance, Who We Are," <http://www.plannedparenthood.org/about-us/who-we-are/pp-services-5552.htm> (May 16, 2008).

4. Janet St. Lawrence, et al, "STD Screening, Testing Case Reporting, and Clinical and Partner Notification Practices: A National Survey of U.S. Physicians," *American Journal of Public Health*, November, 2002, Vol. 92, No. 11.

5. Ibid, p. 312.

6. Vietnamese American Cancer Foundation, "Free Hepatitis B & C Screening," <http://www.ungthu.org/vacf/english/materials/HepBCscreening.asp> (May 29, 2008).

7. Adapted from "Silent Killer: Hepatitis B," by Lisa Liddane, *The Orange County Register*, August 8, 2004 (May 14, 2008).

8. Lisa Marr, M.D., *Sexually Transmitted Diseases: A Physician Tells You What You Need To Know,* Second Edition (Baltimore: The Johns Hopkins University Press, 2007), p. 232.

9. MedicineNet.com, "Ofloxacin," <http://www.medicinenet.com/ofloxacin/article.htm> (May 18, 2008).

10. National Library of Medicine and the National Institutes of Health, MedlinePlus, "Ciprofloxacin," <http://www.nlm.nih.gov/medlineplus/druginfo/medmaster/a688016.html> (May 18, 2008).

11. Marr, p. 236.

12. Gardasil.com, "Important Information about Gardasil," <http://www.gardasil.com/gardasil-information/avaccine-for-cervical-cancer/index/html> (May 18, 2008).

13. Marr, p. 167.

14. Centers for Disease Control and Prevention, "Genital HPV Infection – CDC Fact Sheet," <http://www.cdc.gov/STD/HPV/STDFact-JPV.htm> (May 7, 2008).

Chapter 6: Outlook for the Future

1. Centers for Disease Control and Prevention, "CDC Press Release: 2008 National STD Prevention Conference Draws Nation's Public Health Leaders Together to Confront Sexually Transmitted Diseases," *2008 National STD Prevention Conference*, Chicago, March 10, 2008, <http://www.cdc.gov/stdconference/2008/media/lead-release.htm> (May 26, 2008).

2. National Prevention Information Network, "STD Prevention Today," <http://www.cdcnpin.org/scripts/std/prevent.asp> (May 26, 2008).

3. T. Mueller, et al, "The Association Between Sex Education and Youth's Engagement in Sexual Intercourse, Age at First Intercourse, and Birth Control Use at First Sex," *Journal of Adolescent Health*, Vol. 42, No. 1, January 2008, pp. 89–96, <http://www.jahonline.org/article/PIIS1054139X07003254/fulltext> (May 26, 2008).

4. Jenny Wells, "Safer Sex Practices More Likely Following Mass Media Campaigns," *Medical News Today*, April 11, 2008. <http://www.medicalnewstoday.com/articles/103684.php> (May 26, 2008).

5. Centers for Disease Control and Prevention, "Best Evidence Interventions: Project FIO (The Future is Ours)," *HIV/AIDS Prevention Research Synthesis Project*, (modified: May 7, 2008), <http://www.cdc.gov/hiv/topics/research/prs/resources/factsheets/FIO.htm#ref1> (May 27, 2008).

6. American Psychological Association, "Risky Business: Curbing Adolescent Sexual Behaviors with Interventions," *Psychology Matters*, September 15, 2006, <http://www.psychologymatters.org/riskybusiness.html> (May 27, 2008).

7. Centers for Disease Control and Prevention, "Spotlight: Safe in the City Video Intervention," (modified July 21, 2008), <http://www.cdc.gov/hiv/safeincity.htm> (December 18, 2008).

8. Adapted from "I Have an STD. Now What?" *Cosmopolitan*, December 2007, Vol. 243, No. 6, pp. 206–210.

9. Centers for Disease Control and Prevention, "Evolution of HIV/AIDS Prevention Programs—United States, 1981—2006," *MMWR Weekly*, Vol. 55, No. 21, June 2, 2006, pp. 597–603. <http://www.cdc.gov/mmwr/preview/mmwrhtml/mm5521a4.htm> (May 27, 2008).

10. National HIV and STD Testing Resources. "Frequently Asked Questions," <http://www.hivtest.org/faq.cfm> (May 27, 2008).

11. Food and Drug Administration, "FDA Approves First Home Test for Hepatitis C Virus," *FDA Talk Paper*, April 29, 1999, <http://www.fda.gov/bbs/topics/ANSWERS/ANS00952.html> (May 27, 2008).

12. Centers for Disease Control and Prevention, "Sexually Transmitted Diseases, Legal Status of EPT - Summary Totals," February 26, 2008, <http://www.cdc.gov/std/ept/legal/totals.htm> (May 26, 2008).

13. American Medical Association, "Report 7 of the Council on Science and Public Health (A-06): Expedited Partner Therapy (Patient-delivered Partner Therapy): An Update," <http://www.ama-assn.org/ama/pub/category/16410.html> (June 2006).

14. Herpevac Trial for Women, "Study Overview & FAQs," <http://www.niaid.nih.gov/dmid/stds/herpevac/studyover_faqs.htm> (December 18, 2008).

15. National Cancer Institute, "Human Papillomavirus (HPV) Vaccines: Questions and Answers," (reviewed September 12, 2007), <http://www.cancer.gov/cancertopics/factsheet/Prevention/HPV-vaccine> (December 18, 2008).

16. AIDSinfo: A Service of the U.S. Department of Health and Human Services, "Preventive HIV Vaccines," (reviewed May 2006), <http://www.aidsinfo.nih.gov/ContentFiles/HIVPreventionVaccines_FS_en.pdf> (December 18, 2008).

17. Centers for Disease Control and Prevention, "Availability of Cefixime 400 mg Tablets – United States, April 2008," *MMWR Weekly*, Vol. 57, No. 16, April 25, 2008, p. 435. <http://www.cdc.gov/mmwr/preview/mmwrhtml/mm5716a5.htm?s_cid=mm5716a5_e> (May 27, 2008).

18. AVERT.org, "HIV and AIDS in America," (updated April 7, 2008), <http://www.avert.org/america.htm> (May 27, 2008).

19. AVERT.org, "AIDS around the world," (updated: April 18, 2008). <http://www.avert.org/aroundworld.htm> (May 27, 2008).

Chapter 7: Living With STDs

1. Online conversation with "Carly" (pseudonym), May 14, 2008.

2. Ibid.

3. Ryan White.com, "Ryan's Story," <http://www.ryanwhite.com/pages/story.html.>

4. Ryan White.com, "Ryan's Words," <http://www.ryanwhite.com/pages/words> (May 30, 2008).

5. Society for Human Resource Management, "HIV/AIDS: A Guide for Employers and Managers," <http://www.shrm.org/diversity/AIDSgide/employers.asp> (May 23, 2008).

6. U.S. Department of Education, "Placement of School Children with Acquired Immune Deficiency Syndrome (AIDS)," <http://www.ed.gov/about/offices/list/ocr/docs/hq53e9.html> (May 24, 2008).

7. aidsinfonet.org, "Telling Others You're HIV-Positive," <http://www.aidsinfonet.org/factsheet_detail.php?fsnumber+204&newLang=en> (May 22, 2008).

8. Lisa Marr, M.D., *Sexually Transmitted Diseases: A Physician Tells You What You Need To Know,* Second Edition (Baltimore: The Johns Hopkins University Press, 2007), p. 114.

9. American Social Health Association, "STD/STI Statistics: Fast Facts," <http://www.ashastd.org/learn/learn_statistics.cfm> (March 16, 2008).

10. Online conversation with "Abby" (pseudonym), April 29, 2008.

11. Marr, p. 252.

12. Centers for Disease Control and Prevention, "HIV/AIDS in the United States: All Adults and Adolescents," <http://www.cdc.gov/hiv/resources/factsheets/us/htm> (May 7, 2008).

Glossary

anal sex—Insertion of the penis into a partner's anus.

antibiotic resistance—The ability of a microorganism to resist an antibiotic that was once able to obstruct or destroy it.

antibodies—Protein molecules produced by white blood cells that attack and destroy "foreign" invaders in the body, such as viruses.

AZT—An antiviral drug that stops some retroviruses, such as HIV, from duplicating themselves, and is used to treat AIDS.

biopsy—The removal and examination of a sample of tissue or cells from a body in order to make a diagnosis.

cervix—The narrow, lower end of the uterus that leads to the vagina.

chancre—A primary sore or lesion that forms during the first stage of syphilis and is highly contagious.

chronic—Lasting a long time, often referring to a disease that progresses slowly over a long period of time.

clinical trial—A research study that checks the effectiveness and safety of new medicines or medical devices by testing them on groups of consenting people.

colposcopy—A procedure during which a doctor uses a special magnifying instrument to examine a woman's cervix and vagina for any abnormalities.

combination therapy—A method for treating a disease with two or more drugs or therapies.

congenital—Present before or at birth.

culture—The act of growing living matter, such as bacteria, viruses or tissue, in a medium or substance that cultivates living cells.

DNA—A double-stranded molecule that forms a double helix and determines an individual's hereditary characteristics.

dormant—An inactive state during which growth and development are temporarily suspended.

false negative—An imperfect test result that says what is looked for is not there when it actually is.

false positive—An imperfect test result that says what is looked for is there when it actually is not.

hemophiliac—A person with a genetic disorder that impairs the ability of the blood to clot and often results in excessive bleeding.

infertility—The inability of a couple to achieve a pregnancy after trying for at least one year.

latent—Capable of existing in a host without showing any signs or symptoms of disease.

lubricant—A slippery substance applied to the surface between moving parts to reduce friction.

medium—A substance used to cultivate living cells.

miscarriage—The loss of a fetus before it is able to survive outside the uterus, before the twentieth week of pregnancy.

mucous membrane—The moist lining of any body passage, such as the nose, mouth, or genitals, that comes in contact with the outside and has glands that secrete mucous.

mutation—A structural change in an organism's genes or chromosomes, resulting in a new trait.

opportunistic infections—Secondary infections that appear in people with weakened immune systems, such as with AIDS or after chemotherapy.

oral sex—Stimulation of the male or female genitals using the mouth.

PAP smear—A screening test for cervical cancer during which cells are scraped off the cervix and later examined for abnormalities.

parasite—An organism living in or on another organism from which it gets nourishment, often to the disadvantage of the host organism.

pediculicide—An agent that destroys lice.

penicillin—An antibiotic drug effective against bacteria and used to treat different diseases and infections.

perinatal—Relating to the period around childbirth.

premature—Coming before the expected time, such as a child being born before thirty-seven weeks of pregnancy have passed.

protozoa—A group of single-celled organisms that are usually microscopic.

secretion—A substance that is released from cells or bodily fluids.

spermicide—A preparation, such as a foam or cream, that kills sperm and is used for contraceptive reasons.

unprotected sex—The practice of sex without barriers or protection from STDs and pregnancy.

vaginal intercourse—The penetration of a female's vagina by a male's penis.

virulent—Describing a disease that is extremely infectious, severe, and damaging.

For More Information

Further Reading

Corinna, Heather. *S.E.X.: The All-You-Need-To-Know Progressive Sexuality Guide to Get You Through High School and College.* Cambridge, Mass.: Da Capo Press, 2007.

Currie-McGhee, Leanne. *STDs.* San Diego, Calif.: ReferencePoint Press, 2008.

Grimes, Jill. *Seductive Delusions: How Everyday People Catch STDs.* Baltimore, Md: The Johns Hopkins University Press, 2008.

Hatchell, Deborah. *What Smart Teenagers Know About Dating, Relationships & Sex.* Ventura, Calif.: Piper Books, 2003.

Hyde, Margaret O., and Elizabeth H. Forsyth. *Safe Sex 101: An Overview for Teens.* Minneapolis, Minn.: Twenty-First Century Books, 2006.

Libby, Roger W. *The Naked Truth About Sex: A Guide to Intelligent Sexual Choices for Teenagers and Twentysomethings.* Topanga, Calif.: Freedom Press, 2006.

Internet Addresses

The Nemours Foundation. © 1995–2008. *KidsHealth.* <http://www.kidshealth.com/>

Planned Parenthood® Federation of America. © 1999–2008. *Teenwire.com.* <http://www.teenwire.com/>

U.S. Department of Health and Human Services. *AIDSinfo.* <http://www.aidsinfo.nih.gov/>

Organizations

American Social Health Association (ASHA)
P.O. Box 13827
Research Triangle Park, NC 27709
(800) 227-8922
<http://www.ashastd.org/>

Black AIDS Institute
1833 W 8th St, Suite 200
Los Angeles, CA 90057
(213) 353-3610
<http://www.blackaids.org/>

Centers for Disease Control and Prevention (CDC)
National Prevention Information Network
P.O. Box 6003
Rockville, MD 20849
(800) 458-5231
<http://www.cdcnpin.org/scripts/index.asp>

Hepatitis B Foundation
3805 Old Easton Road
Doylestown, PA 18902
(215) 489-4900
<http://www.hepb.org/>

National Cervical Cancer Coalition (NCCC)
6520 Platt Ave. #693
West Hills, CA 91307
(800) 685-5531
<http://www.nccc-online.org/>

Planned Parenthood® Federation of America
1110 Vermont Ave. NW
Washington, DC 20005
(800) 230-7526
<http://www.plannedparenthood.org/>

Index